I0448271

EP-FB

Comptroller of the Currency
Administrator of National Banks

Federal Branches and Agencies Supervision

Comptroller's Handbook

December 1999

Federal Branches/Agencies

Table of Contents

Introduction

Background   1
Laws, Regulations, and Rulings   3
Supervision by Risk   5
    Risk Definitions   7
    Risk Management   8
Measuring and Assessing Risk   10
    Core Assessment   11
    Risk Assessment System   12
    ROCA Assessment   13
The Supervision Process   14
    FBO Supervision Program   17
    Supervisory Actions and Enforcement 20
    Communication with Foreign Bank Supervisors   23

Special Considerations

Capital Equivalency Deposit Account   25
Regulatory Reports   27
Record Keeping   28
Operations Booked at Other FBO Offices   28

Risk Management Issues

Management and Supervision   31
Asset Quality and Internal Loan Review   32
Small Business Loans   34
Concentrations of Credit   35
Allowance for Loan and Lease Losses   36
Asset/Liability Management   37
Liquidity   39
Trading Activities   41
Earnings   42
Internal Controls and Audit   42

Other Examination Issues

Private Banking   45
Due-To/From Head Office Account   47
Compliance   48

Appendices

A. Core Assessment   50
B. Risk Assessment System   89
C. Risk Matrix   124
D. ROCA Rating System   125

Glossary   135

References   138

Background

Foreign banking organizations (FBOs) have long conducted banking operations in the United States through branches, agencies, and subsidiaries. With the passage of the International Banking Act (IBA) in 1978, foreign banks could opt to conduct banking operations through a branch or agency licensed by the Comptroller of the Currency (12 USC 3101-3111). Such licensed entities are known as "federal branches and agencies." ("State branches and agencies" are licensed by the states and supervised by them and the Federal Reserve System.) Federal branches and agencies can exercise much the same rights and privileges as national banks and are subject to much the same laws, rulings, and regulations. The principle behind this consistency of treatment is termed national treatment.

A federal branch is an FBO's office licensed by the OCC to exercise such banking powers as accepting deposits and operating as a fiduciary. (To be a fiduciary, a federal branch or agency must obtain a separate approval.) Before 1991, insured federal branches (like insured state branches) could accept both retail and wholesale deposits. The Federal Deposit Insurance Corporation Improvement Act (FDICIA) of 1991 prohibited these branches from accepting deposits of less than $100,000. A grandfathering provision permits insured federal branches in existence on the date of FDICIA's enactment to continue accepting insured deposits of less than $100,000. (See also "limited federal branch" in this booklet's glossary.)

A federal agency is an FBO's office that is licensed by the OCC to engage in the business of banking but not to accept deposits or exercise fiduciary powers. Agencies primarily make commercial and corporate loans and finance international transactions. Although a federal agency cannot accept deposits, it can maintain credit balances. Such balances must be:

- Incidental to, or must arise from the exercise of, other lawful banking powers.

- For a specific purpose.

- Withdrawn within a reasonable period of time after the specific purpose for their placement has been accomplished. Such balances must be drawn upon in a reasonable manner based on the size and nature of the account.

Such balances must not be:

- Solicited from the general public.

- Used to pay routine operating expenses in the United States.

Subject to statutory restrictions, the OCC may modify the rules for federal branches and agencies to promote safety and soundness and to maintain competitive equality between federal branches/agencies and national banks.

Most federal branches and agencies operate in major U.S. cities, where international trade and finance flourishes. Most federal branches and agencies are wholesale operations engaged in trade and corporate financing. Most obtain their funding from interbank markets and related parties. A few conduct retail operations and are insured by the Federal Deposit Insurance Corporation (FDIC). All are exposed to much the same risks as domestic banks and should be supervised with the same skill and judgment as national banks.

To promote nationwide consistency in the application of OCC's examination policies and practices, the agency consolidates supervision of all federal branches and agencies in its Northeastern District. On-site examinations are generally performed by examiners working at duty stations in proximity to the federal branch or agency. These examiners are usually experienced in federal branch and agency examinations. The OCC also participates in the Interagency Foreign Banking Organization Supervision Program (FBO Supervision Program) developed by federal and state banking regulators to strengthen the supervision of U.S. operations of FBOs.

The International Banking and Finance Division (IB&F) in Washington, D.C., supports the supervision of federal branches and agencies by coordinating OCC's participation in the FBO Supervision Program, developing supervisory policy, advising on international financial developments affecting FBOs and their home countries, and coordinating communication with foreign bank supervisors.

The supervisory approach in this booklet is risk-based and is modeled on the OCC's Large Bank Supervision Program. This booklet does not provide guidance for examining specific activities or products. Examiners should refer to other booklets in the Comptroller's Handbook for relevant examination procedures. The purpose of this booklet is to:

- Articulate supervision-by-risk policies as they apply to federal branches and agencies. (Such policies include core assessment and risk assessment system (RAS) guidelines.)

- Explain operational aspects of the OCC's supervision of federal branches and agencies in the context of the FBO Supervision Program.

- Highlight special considerations arising from legal and operational structures that differentiate federal branches and agencies from national banks.

- Define terms commonly used in the supervision of the U.S. operations of FBOs.

Laws, Regulations, and Rulings

Pursuant to the IBA, a federal branch or agency has the same rights and responsibilities as a national bank operating at the same location. Thus, as a general rule, federal branches and agencies are subject to the same laws as national banks. The IBA states, however, that this general rule does not apply when the IBA or other applicable law provides other specific standards for federal branches or agencies, or when the OCC determines that the general rule should not apply.

The IBA's general rule expresses the so-called "national treatment" or nondiscrimination principle that seeks to ensure competitive equality between foreign and domestic banks. Because there are structural and organizational differences between U.S. banks and foreign banks, however, national treatment does not mean that in each instance a supervisory agency should mechanically apply to federal branches and agencies the same standard that it applies to national banks. In some instances, the agency should apply different rules to federal branches and agencies to ensure functionally equal treatment. For example, federal branches and agencies are required to maintain Capital

Equivalency Deposit Accounts (CEDs) as described in the "CED Account" section of this booklet.

When laws or OCC regulations and rulings do not provide a specific rule for federal branches and agencies, the OCC makes a determination as to their applicability to federal branches and agencies. It should be understood that many statutory requirements only apply to institutions that engage in the activities addressed by the statute. Thus, for example, consumer laws would normally apply only to federal branches or agencies that engage in the consumer banking activity specified in the statute in question. Similarly, fiduciary requirements would apply only to federal branches that exercise fiduciary powers. The Bank Secrecy Act and its implementing regulation (BSA) apply to both national banks and federal branches and agencies, but certain risks or activities are more likely to occur in federal branches and agencies. Examiners should review the "Bank Secrecy Act" booklet of the Comptroller's Handbook for guidance on compliance with BSA regulations and other money-laundering laws.

In other instances, a legal analysis of the statute may indicate that the statute was not intended to apply to foreign bank branches, as in the case of 12 USC 371c (regarding restrictions on transactions with the parent foreign bank). Also, certain statutes stating that they apply to insured depository institutions frequently raise questions about their applicability to uninsured federal branches and agencies. In many cases, safe and sound banking practices endorsed by the OCC may require that the same standard apply to uninsured branches and agencies.

In the past, the OCC has reviewed a number of questions about the applicability of laws and regulations to federal branches and agencies. The agency has issued interpretations of these statutes. If uncertain whether a given law or regulation applies to a federal branch or agency, examiners should check previous interpretations or consult with their district counsel.

Supervision by Risk

The OCC's objectives for the supervision of federal branches and agencies are to:

• Determine the condition of the federal branch or agency and the risks associated with current and planned activities, taking into account, as appropriate, risks originating from its head office, related offices, and the home country financial environment.

- Evaluate the overall integrity and effectiveness of risk management systems, periodically validating the systems using transaction testing.

- Enforce banking laws and regulation.

- Communicate findings, recommendations, and requirements to federal branch or agency management and, as appropriate, to head office management in a clear and timely manner. OCC examiners should also obtain informal or formal commitments to correct significant deficiencies.

- Verify the effectiveness of corrective supervisory actions, or, if supervisory actions have not been undertaken or accomplished, pursue resolution through more aggressive supervision or enforcement actions. Supervisory actions may include the involvement of head office management and home country bank supervisors.

- Coordinate with the Federal Reserve System and other U.S. regulators, when appropriate, to enhance the effectiveness of consolidated supervision of U.S. operations of FBOs.

In risk profile, federal branches and agencies resemble large national banks more closely than they do community banks because they are often part of large, internationally active FBOs. These FBOs have intricate legal and financial structures and offer sophisticated products and services. The risks assumed by federal branch or agency management are part of the parent FBO's global business strategy. The OCC therefore applies OCC's large bank supervisory policies to federal branches and agencies to the extent practical.

By using these large bank policies, the OCC is better able to identify and evaluate internal and external risks to a federal branch or agency. The operational and financial stability of federal branches and agencies depends on the support of their head offices or, absent that, the support of their home country financial authorities. Therefore, any assessment of a federal branch's or agency's condition must take into account the financial strength of the FBO and the home country's financial environment. OCC supervisory practices for federal branch and agency supervision reflect this focus, in addition to providing a risk-based examination approach tailored to the structural characteristics of federal branches and agencies. IB&F staff has developed a variety of written products that inform OCC examiners about current developments related to the home country's economic environment, financial system, and banking sector. OCC examiners can obtain these products through the IB&F intranet site.

Under OCC's supervision by risk approach, examiners do not attempt to prohibit risk-taking. Rather, they attempt to ensure that local and head office senior management understand the types and levels of risks undertaken at the federal branch or agency. They determine whether the federal branch's or agency's risk management systems effectively identify, measure, control, and monitor its internal risks. When risk is not properly managed, the OCC directs the federal branch's or agency's management and, if necessary, head office senior management to take corrective action. Always, the OCC is concerned that the federal branch or agency has the necessary managerial and financial support from the FBO to meet its obligations and otherwise operate on a safe and sound basis. When the head office's support is weak, the OCC may need to apply supervisory restrictions or other measures to protect the interests of depositors and creditors.

Supervision by risk allocates greater resources to areas with higher risks. The OCC accomplishes this by:

- Identifying risk using common definitions. The categories of risk, as defined, are the foundation for supervisory activities.

- Measuring risk using common methods of evaluation. Risk cannot always be quantified in dollars. For example, numerous internal control deficiencies may indicate excessive transaction risk.

- Evaluating risk management to determine whether the federal branch's or agency's systems adequately manage and control existing levels of risk.

- Performing examinations based on the core assessment or other optional procedures, reaching conclusions on the risk profile and condition of the federal branch or agency, and following up on areas of supervisory concern.

To accomplish these tasks, examiners discuss preliminary conclusions regarding risks with federal branch or agency management, adjusting those conclusions, if appropriate. The OCC can then focus supervisory efforts on significant risks, i.e., the areas of highest risk affecting the federal branch or agency.

Examiners establish the risk profile of the federal branch or agency to document the financial condition at the U.S. operation, compliance with U.S. law and regulations, and the protection of depositors and creditors. Examiners determine whether the FBO's financial condition and the home country's financial circumstances mitigate or accentuate concerns about this risk profile.

Risk Definitions

The OCC assesses banking risk relative to its impact on capital and earnings. From a supervisory perspective, risk is the potential that events, expected or unanticipated, may have an adverse impact on the bank's capital or earnings. But because federal branches and agencies are not separately capitalized and their earnings performance has only a partial impact on the overall revenue stream of the FBO, the risks they take should be ultimately considered in light of the support provided by their FBO or home country financial authorities.

The OCC has defined nine categories of risk for bank supervision purposes. These risks are: credit, interest rate, liquidity, price, foreign currency translation, transaction, compliance, strategic, and reputation risk. These categories are not mutually exclusive; any product or service may expose the federal branch or agency to multiple risks. For purposes of analysis and discussion, however, the OCC identifies and assesses the risks separately. The risk definitions are found in appendix B, "Risk Assessment System."

For risk exposures that may be under the control of federal branch or agency management, the applicable risks should be evaluated using OCC examination guidance. The evaluation of the federal branch's or agency's risk exposures and risk management processes should focus as much as possible on the adequacy of the federal branch's or agency's risk management systems and whether they work well with the FBO's risk management systems.

Risk Management

Market conditions and the structures of FBOs and their federal branches and agencies vary; therefore, there is no single risk management system that works for all federal branches and agencies. Each institution should tailor its risk management program to its needs and circumstances. Adequate risk management systems can vary in sophistication depending on the size of the federal branch or agency and the complexity of its operations. Sound risk management systems, however, have several characteristics in common. Regardless of the risk management program's design, each program should:

- Identify risk: To properly identify risks, federal branch or agency management must recognize and understand existing risks or risks that may arise from new business initiatives. Risk identification should be a continuing process and should occur at both the transaction and portfolio level.

- Measure risk: Accurate and timely measurement of risks is essential to effective risk management systems. If the federal branch or agency does not have an adequate risk management system, federal branch or agency management has limited its ability to control risk levels or allow head office management to monitor them. The more complex the risk, the more sophisticated should be the tools that measure it. Federal branch or agency management should periodically test to make sure that the measurement tools it uses are accurate. Good risk measurement systems assess the risks of both individual transactions and portfolios. They are independent of risk-taking activities.

- Control risk: Federal branch or agency management should adhere to the FBO's risk limits communicated by head office management through policies, standards, and procedures that define responsibility and authority. These control limits are valid head office management tools, adjusted when conditions or risk tolerances change. The management of the federal branch or agency should have a process in place that authorizes exceptions or changes to risk limits when warranted.

- Monitor risk: Federal branch or agency management should have in place a process to ensure timely review of risk positions and exceptions and permit head office management review. Monitoring reports should be frequent, timely, accurate, and informative and should be distributed to appropriate individuals to ensure action, when needed.

To manage the federal branch's or agency's risk effectively, head office management must be informed, local management must be capable, and staffing must be appropriate. Head office management must establish the federal branch's or agency's strategic direction and risk tolerances. In carrying out these responsibilities, head office senior management should approve policies that set standards (e.g., on risk tolerances). Well-designed monitoring systems will allow head office senior management to hold federal branch or agency management accountable for operating within established tolerances.

Capable management and appropriate staffing are critical to effective risk management. Attention should be given to retaining and recruiting capable executives, line managers, risk management personnel, and back-office staff. Head office management should establish policies and procedures to ensure the timely and orderly succession of branch management. Federal branch or agency management is responsible for the implementation, integrity, and maintenance of risk management systems. Federal branch or agency management must put in place effective risk management systems to:

- Implement the FBO's strategic direction;

- Implement policies that put into practice the FBO's risk tolerances and strategic goals;

- Ensure that strategic direction and risk tolerances are effectively communicated and are adhered to by appropriate federal branch or agency personnel; and

- Keep head office management informed of federal branch or agency operations;

- Oversee the development and maintenance of management information systems to ensure that information is timely, accurate, pertinent, and adequately reported to head office management.

When examiners assess risk management systems at federal branches or agencies, they consider the policies, processes, personnel, and control systems put in place by local and head office management to operate the federal branch or agency. If any one of these areas is deficient, so is the federal branch's or agency's management processes. For more detailed definitions of policies, processes, personnel, and control systems, see the "Bank Supervision Process" and "Large Bank Supervision" booklets of the Comptroller's Handbook.

Measuring and Assessing Risk

Using the OCC's RAS for federal branches and agencies as a guide, an examiner obtains both a current and prospective view of a federal branch's or agency's risk profile. The core assessment standards guide examiners to conclusions regarding the nine categories of risk and ROCA ratings. The RAS and core assessment standards used for federal branches and agencies are modifications of those used for large bank supervision. Risk assessments drive supervisory strategies and activities, and facilitate discussions with federal branch and agency management to ensure more efficient examinations.

The risk assessments should also factor in significant political, economic, and banking sector developments in the FBO's home country. Examiners should also recognize the limitations of the RAS, since the federal branch or agency is only a part of the FBO. Examiners should recognize that the analysis of the FBO's ability to serve as a source of support is a key element in the risk assessment of the federal branch or agency. (Such an analysis is described in the "FBO Supervision Program" section of this booklet.) Examiners should recognize that weak accounting, supervisory, and disclosure regimes in many countries limit the ability of U.S. bank supervisors to reach conclusions on the evolving condition of some FBOs.

An effective risk measurement system calculates dollars at risk relative to earnings or capital. Because federal branches and agencies have no segregated capital base and are only part of the FBO's earnings stream, measurement of capital at risk is not meaningful for federal branches and agencies. Nevertheless, appropriate systems should be in place that enable federal branch and agency management, as well as FBO management, to estimate in dollars the branch's or agency's exposure to such forces as changing interest rates, price levels, and market conditions. Management should also be able to monitor the branch's or agency's compliance with limits set by the FBO.

Core Assessment

Core assessment standards are the minimum conclusions that must be reached during the designated supervisory cycle for low-risk areas of federal branches and agencies. The core assessment standards are detailed in appendix A. Core assessment standards are designed to ensure that examiner judgment and discretion are preserved, while establishing a consistent set of required considerations. The inherent flexibility of the core assessment standards allows for the application of the standards to federal branches and agencies to the extent practical. Using these standards, examiners may assess risks for all product lines.

When using the core assessment standards, examiners should use judgment in deciding how to work through the considerations and how much independent testing is needed. Examiners should be alert to specific activities or risks that may require the examiner-in-charge (EIC) to broaden the scope of the examination. Examiners are encouraged to expand the examination procedures to include the optional procedures outlined in other Comptroller's Handbook booklets when risks are increasing or activities are complex.

The core assessment standards are designed to complement the RAS and include minimum standards for each risk category. Given the importance of a strong internal control culture, the OCC has also defined standards for internal controls that contain the minimum conclusions examiners should reach regarding each federal branch's or agency's control environment.

Risk Assessment System

By completing the core assessment and, as necessary, other more detailed procedures, examiners assess the risk exposure for the nine categories of risk using the RAS framework (see appendix B). For seven of the risks – credit, interest rate, liquidity, price, foreign currency translation, transaction, and compliance, the RAS concisely documents judgments regarding the quantity of risk, the quality of risk management, the level of supervisory concern (measured as aggregate or composite risk), and the direction of risk.

The remaining categories of risk are strategic risk and reputation risk. Because these risks affect the FBO's franchise value, examiners must assess them. Because these risks are difficult to quantify, examiners must modify the assessment, evaluating the "composite risk" and the "direction of risk" based on conclusions from the core assessment.

The methods used to assess the quantity of risk, quality of risk management, aggregate risk, direction of risk, and composite risk for federal branches and agencies are the same as described in the "Bank Supervision Process" and "Large Bank Supervision" booklets of the Comptroller's Handbook.

Using their assessments of the nine categories of risk under the RAS framework, examiners establish an overall risk profile of the federal branch or agency. Examiners should update the risk profile at least quarterly (more frequently if district office management requires). Conclusions drawn from the risk assessments of federal branches or agencies are captured in OCC's electronic information system. (See appendix C for a table showing how assessments of quantity of risk and quality of risk management converge.)

By including information on the FBO and its home country financial environment in the evaluation of each federal branch or agency, an examiner can gain a clearer picture of the risks facing the federal branch or agency. The relative importance of identified risks influences the development of the strategy and the assignment of resources.

ROCA Assessment

The ROCA rating system for federal branches and agencies is analogous to the CAMELS rating system for national banks. Unlike CAMELS, ROCA does not explicitly rate capital, earnings, and liquidity; in these areas, a federal branch or agency cannot be evaluated separately from the FBO.

The ROCA system rates four areas: Risk Management, Operational Controls, Compliance, and Asset Quality (ROCA). The system places the highest priority on risk management. The composite rating should indicate the overall condition of the federal branch or agency. (See the ROCA discussion in appendix D for a detailed description of rating standards.)

The emphasis on risk management enables examiners (1) to incorporate the principles of supervision by risk into the federal branch or agency evaluation and (2) to recognize how management (both local and at the head office), policies, processes, and practices affect the current and future condition of the federal branch or agency. The operational controls rating includes internal controls and internal/external audit activities. The compliance rating reflects compliance with safety and soundness regulations, as well as consumer regulations, for federal branches and agencies offering products covered under consumer laws. Examiners should also enter a separate consumer compliance rating in OCC's electronic information system.

Under the ROCA ratings system, the evaluation of asset quality helps examiners to assess the effectiveness of credit risk management. It is also an indication of the value of the federal branch's or agency's asset base in the event of liquidation. When examiners are confident about the ability and willingness of the FBO's management to support the federal branch or agency, the evaluation of asset quality may have less priority. The asset quality rating depends on the volume of problem assets. Adequacy of credit administration is included in the risk management rating. Asset quality at an offshore branch managed by federal branch or agency management should not affect the asset quality rating. If examiners are concerned about the management of offshore assets at the federal branch or agency, the concerns can be reflected in the risk management rating.

The ROCA system is also designed to work in harmony with the FBO Supervision Program, particularly the joint process of preparing an overall rating of the consolidated U.S. operations of each FBO. In addition, when the ROCA rating is considered in conjunction with the strength of support assessment (SOSA) prepared for each FBO, examiners will be better equipped to judge the FBO's ability to support the federal branch or agency from a financial and managerial point of view. The combined assessment of an FBO's U.S. operations and the SOSA are described in the "FBO Supervision Program" section of this booklet. These tools can help examiners set the scope of on-site examinations and off-site monitoring; they also help examiners judge whether supervisory and enforcement actions are appropriate.

The Supervision Process

The supervision of federal branches and agencies is a cyclical process. While the planning, examining, and communication processes used for large banks are generally applicable, they should be applied in a way that reflects the operational differences of federal branches and agencies. OCC supervisory processes should take into account that each federal branch or agency is part of an FBO. In addition, the multiple bank supervisory jurisdictions over U.S. operations of FBOs require the OCC to coordinate its supervisory activities with the Federal Reserve System, FDIC, and state bank supervisors. This coordination is governed by the FBO program discussed in the "FBO Supervision Program" section of this booklet. The "Bank Supervision Process," "Large Bank Supervision," and "Examination Planning and Control" booklets of the Comptroller's Handbook provide guidance on the planning, examining, and communication processes as they relate to federal branches and agencies.

The purpose of planning is to develop detailed strategies for effectively and efficiently supervising each federal branch or agency. Planning begins with a careful and thoughtful assessment of a federal branch's or agency's current and anticipated risks. In this regard, examiners should understand head office management's strategic purpose in establishing the federal branch or agency. Examiners should also gain some understanding about the FBO, its home country economic environment, and developments there that may affect its operation. The financial and managerial support provided by the FBO is given important consideration.

Examiners maintain communication with other OCC examiners or other supervisory agencies to help coordinate supervision of FBOs' U.S. operations. (See also "Communication with Foreign Bank Supervisors" section of this booklet.) Planning also requires effective and periodic communication with federal branch or agency management, and senior head office management where necessary. Through discussions with federal branch or agency management, examiners can help confirm that supervisory resources are directed at the areas of highest risk.

Supervisory strategies direct examination activities. Examiners gain a fundamental understanding of the condition of the federal branch or agency, the quality of management, and control afforded by risk management systems. A primary objective of federal branch and agency examinations is to verify the integrity of internal risk management systems, including systems for reporting to head office senior management. Supervisory strategies are developed by the EIC, reviewed and approved by district management, and documented in the OCC's electronic information system. For FBOs operating multiple federal branches or agencies, consolidated strategies are appropriate. Additional guidance on establishing supervisory strategies can be found in the "Large Bank Supervision" and "Bank Supervision Process" booklets of the Comptroller's Handbook.

The frequency of federal branch and agency on-site safety and soundness examinations is governed by 12 CFR 4.7. Every federal branch or agency must receive a full-scope, on-site examination no less than once every 12 months. This time period may be extended to 18 months if a federal branch or agency meets the following criteria:

- Has total assets of $250 million or less.

- Has received a composite ROCA supervisory rating of 1 or 2 at its most recent examination.

- Satisfies one of the following requirements:

  - In the FBO's most recent report on its capital adequacy position, it has Tier 1 (or equivalent) capital of 6 percent and total risk-based capital of 10 percent on a consolidated basis.
  - Federal branch or agency management has maintained on a daily basis, over the past three quarters, eligible assets (their eligibility determined by applicable federal and state law) in an amount not less than 108 percent of the preceding quarter's average third-party liabilities, and sufficient liquidity is currently available to meet obligations to third parties (third-party liabilities are defined in this booklet's glossary).

- Is not subject to a formal enforcement action or order.

- Has not experienced a change in control during the preceding 12-month period in which a full-scope, on-site examination would have been required. For purposes of this rule, a federal branch or agency will be deemed to have undergone a change in control if it is sold to another foreign bank or if the foreign bank that owns it has undergone a change in control.

The OCC has the discretion to conduct exams more frequently if circumstances warrant. Such circumstances include changes in the level or direction of risk in a federal branch or agency or in the level of third-party liabilities.

Federal branch or agency management must receive a Report of Examination (ROE) once every supervisory cycle. The ROE communicates the overall condition of the federal branch or agency, summarizing examiners' activities during the most recent supervisory cycle and incorporating their findings. The ROE also identifies the root causes of any significant deficiencies examiners identified and assesses the effectiveness of any corrective action plans established for the federal branch or agency, including how well the plans were executed.

Examiners should use the uniform common core report of examination for national banks, as adapted for the examination of a federal branch or agency by the district office. Exceptions are permitted when other communications with the federal branch or agency clearly communicate the composite and component ROCA ratings and review the significant risks. When alternate communications are used and copies provided to the other financial institution regulators, the correspondence should be sufficiently informative.

OCC's Electronic Information System

On the OCC's electronic information system, examiners record the current condition, supervisory strategy, and supervisory concerns for each federal branch or agency. They also document follow-up actions, management discussions, commitments to corrective action, progress in correcting identified problems, and subsequent events. The EIC is responsible for ensuring that the electronic files for federal branches and agencies are accurate and up-to-date. Using these electronic records, OCC senior management reviews the condition of individual federal branches or the system as a group. Other federal bank supervisors also have access to the system.

FBO Supervision Program

The FBO Supervision Program, operated jointly by the Federal Reserve System, FDIC, OCC, and state bank supervisors, strengthens the oversight of the U.S. activities of FBOs and the coordination among U.S. bank supervisors. Through the program, the U.S. bank supervisors share information with each other as well as the home country supervisors of FBOs. While the principle behind the FBO Supervision Program is shared authority (among all participating federal and state bank supervisors), the OCC maintains its regulatory, supervisory, and examination authority over federal branches and agencies. Foreign-owned national banks are also covered under the program.

Each year, participating supervisors draft supervision strategies for the U.S. operations of individual FBOs. In developing these strategies, regulators assess the overall condition of the combined U.S. operations of the FBO. To support this activity, regulators assess the financial ability of the FBO to support its U.S. operations. When doing so, they prepare a SOSA for the FBO.

Comprehensive Examination Plan

An annual comprehensive examination plan (CEP) is developed for each FBO that has more than one entity operating in the United States. The appropriate supervisory authority develops the examination plan with input from all the supervisory agencies involved in the supervision of the FBO's U.S. operations. Generally, examinations are scheduled so that the multiple offices, including national bank subsidiaries of the FBO, are examined using the same examination date.

OCC coordination with the appropriate Federal Reserve bank is necessary when the FBO operates a mix of state and federally licensed entities. To the extent possible, examination plans should include national and state subsidiary banks of the FBO and attempt to coordinate "as of" dates.

The goal of the CEP is to coordinate simultaneous examinations of each of an FBO's U.S. activities (including all state or federal branches and agencies, all state or national banks, and all other affiliated nonbank operations or organizations). Under the FBO Supervision Program, relevant federal and state bank supervisors will coordinate simultaneous examinations. When the examinations are completed, the OCC will produce and distribute its own report of examination for each federal branch, agency, or national bank involved in the simultaneous examination.

Combined Assessment of U.S. Operations

When the examination of the FBO's operations is concluded, an overall assessment is made of the combined operations of all of the parts of the FBO's U.S. operations, including branches, agencies, representative offices, and bank and nonbanking subsidiaries. The overall assessment is communicated to head office senior management through a summary of condition letter. A copy of the letter is provided to the home country supervisor. The letters are drafted 60 days after the examinations of the FBO's U.S. offices are completed. The OCC is responsible for preparing summary of condition letters for FBOs that operate in the United States through federal branches or agencies or through a mix of OCC and state-licensed operations (provided the state-licensed operations are not significant). The OCC will provide input on summary of condition letters prepared by the Federal Reserve banks that address the U.S. operations of FBOs and include federal branches, agencies, or national banks.

The combined assessment, which is based on the input of, and examinations conducted by, federal or state supervisors, will produce an overall single-component rating between "1" and "5" for the combined U.S. operations. A rating of "1" represents fundamentally sound operations and a "5" represents unsafe and unsound conditions. If the assessment identifies "systemic" problems or other issues of general concern, it may trigger administrative action against the federal branch or agency, or it could lead to other supervisory follow-up with the FBO. Enforcement and supervisory follow-up for the individual U.S. operations of the FBO remains the responsibility of the primary regulator of each U.S. operation.

Strength of Support Assessment

The FBO Supervision Program is focused on assessing the financial and managerial support that each FBO provides to its U.S. operations. This assessment helps the supervisor of each U.S. component of an FBO decide on the scope of examinations, as well as the nature and type of follow-up, including enforcement actions and other supervisory initiatives. The SOSA reflects the overall financial condition of the FBO, its managerial and operational record, the system of supervision in its home country, the economic environment and financial system in which it operates, and other pertinent factors, including a judgment on the FBO's ability to maintain adequate internal controls and compliance procedures at its U.S. offices.

Using the results of the SOSA, examiners assign the FBO a rating from "A" to "E." The "A" rating represents the lowest level of supervisory concern and "E" the highest. An asterisk is appended to the SOSA rating if examiners have any concerns about the ability of the FBO to maintain adequate internal controls and compliance procedures at its U.S. offices, regardless of the FBO's overall condition. The reasons for such concerns could be a recent merger, rapid expansion in new types of business or geographic areas, or publicized control problems at non-U.S. operations that could pose a risk to the U.S. operations. Although such circumstances may not immediately change the FBO's overall financial profile, they indicate that existing or potential weaknesses unrelated to the FBO's ability to meet its financial obligations need to be taken into account when assessing the FBO's U.S. operations. The SOSA rating is confidential and for the supervisors' internal use only; it is not disclosed to the FBO or the home country supervisor. Examiners should take into account the findings in SOSAs as they formulate strategies and supervisory activities at federal branches and agencies.

FBO Desktop

The FBO Desktop is an automated electronic system designed and maintained by the Federal Reserve Board to facilitate information-sharing and collaboration in the supervision of foreign institutions. The OCC distributes work products to the Federal Reserve System and other participants in the FBO Supervision Program through the FBO Desktop. These products include SOSAs, reviews of home country financial systems and accounting practices, examination plans, summary of condition letters, and trip reports about countries that interest FBO program participants.

Supervisory Actions and Enforcement

The wide range of supervisory and enforcement tools addressing violations of laws and regulations and breaches of safety and soundness in national banks can usually be used in federal branches and agencies. These tools include: moral suasion, commitment letters, memoranda of understanding (MOU), formal agreements, cease and desist (C&D) orders (including temporary orders), and orders of investigation. The OCC may remove federal branch or agency management and assess civil money penalties. In certain circumstances, the OCC may also terminate a federal branch or agency license at its own initiative or at the recommendation of the Federal Reserve Board.

In recent years, the OCC has employed these tools to address unsafe and unsound practices at individual federal branches or agencies. The OCC has also taken supervisory actions when questions arose about the ability of FBOs to support their federal branches or agencies and when the FBOs' home countries were in significant economic turmoil. The OCC's supervisory and enforcement actions are taken after a case-by-case evaluation of the facts and circumstances. The Northeastern District Office is responsible for taking supervisory and enforcement actions in consultation with IB&F, the Law Department, and such specialty units as the action may require.

Supervisory concerns over risk management, operational controls, and compliance with U.S. laws at individual federal branches or agencies can be addressed through specific provisions in supervisory follow-up actions. The severity of the action would depend on the seriousness of the problems as well as the cooperation and receptivity of local and head office management. Generally speaking, a composite ROCA rating of 3 or worse would trigger consideration of some form of supervisory action.

An FBO's strength of support assessment may also raise supervisory concerns. Weak home country supervision and support, an increasing level of country risk, and weak internal controls within the FBO can each diminish an FBO's ability to support its U.S. operations financially or managerially. When imposing a supervisory action because an FBO's support is not sufficient, the OCC should consider a variety of measures. These may include: maintenance of eligible assets; limits on net due-from head and related offices' balances; minimum (short-term) liquidity positions; capital equivalency deposits (CEDs) above minimum levels and made up of greater-than-normal amounts of liquid and higher-quality assets; and limits on balance sheet growth and transactions with related parties. A key objective in these supervisory actions is to ensure that sufficient (liquid and good-quality) assets are maintained at the federal branch or agency to honor any third-party liabilities and to ensure that head office management will provide sufficient managerial support, if necessary.

OCC's supervisory and enforcement actions have been effective in correcting deficiencies at individual federal branches and agencies and addressing concerns over the strength of support provided by the FBO. The use of asset maintenance and liquidity requirements in supervisory actions has generally led to stronger federal branch or agency liquidity and greater asset coverage of third-party liabilities. Such actions increase the likelihood that third-party creditors would be repaid in the event the federal branch or agency has to be liquidated using only its assets.

The OCC can ensure that the federal branch or agency maintains sufficient assets to cover third-party liabilities by effecting certain agreements with it. An asset maintenance agreement (12 CFR 28.20) customarily requires the federal branch or agency to maintain a specified percentage of designated assets to third-party liabilities. A liquidity maintenance agreement usually requires a ratio of liquid assets to third-party liabilities and a specific coverage for future maturity periods. (In such agreements, the OCC would define which assets are eligible for inclusion in the computations.)

In certain circumstances, the OCC may need to apply the prompt corrective action (PCA) requirements under 12 CFR 6 to address serious deficiencies. The PCA requirements apply only to federal branches insured by the FDIC. The OCC employs the FDIC's asset pledge and asset maintenance requirements (12 CFR 346) to determine insured federal branches' PCA compliance. PCA directives take effect when an insured federal branch's pledged asset ratio falls below 5 percent or its asset maintenance ratio falls below 106 percent. An insured federal branch's noncompliance with the minimum asset pledge and the asset maintenance requirements may signal either a serious disregard for U.S. law on the part of local or head office management or solvency/liquidity problems at the FBO. In such cases, under 12 CFR 6, the OCC may issue a PCA directive. While directives to national banks (e.g., on capital distributions, management fees to controlling owners, capital restoration plans, and asset growth and expansion) may serve as a model, PCA directives should be tailored to fit the federal branch's circumstances.

In the past, questions have arisen about who should sign supervisory actions for a federal branch or agency. Although exceptions may be necessary in particular circumstances, the following guidelines usually apply:

- For informal actions, the signatories should be federal branch or agency management and appropriate head office senior management. The head office representative would not usually be required to travel to the United States to sign the document. Federal branch or agency management may transmit the document to the head office for signature. The OCC will accept the signature of a senior head office manager acting on behalf of the FBO's board of directors without requiring authentication of the signature.

- For formal actions, representatives of the FBO's board of directors (either a senior bank officer specifically authorized by the board or a member of the board) should normally travel to the OCC Northeastern District Office to discuss and sign the document. If there are compelling reasons why the representative cannot travel, the signature on the enforcement document must be authenticated by a consular official at the U.S. embassy in the home country of the FBO.

Communication with Foreign Bank Supervisors

Communication with foreign bank supervisors is common in the supervision of federal branches and agencies. Foreign bank supervisors can be a valuable source of information on the condition and operation of the FBO and may be helpful in reinforcing the institution of sound risk management practices throughout the FBO. The OCC maintains written agreements or understandings with several domestic and foreign regulators that cover the types of communication that can be shared, confidentiality requirements, and reciprocity. Examiners should be aware of existing written information-sharing agreements, as well as PPMs and laws governing cooperation and information-sharing with other regulators. PPM 5500-1 and the "Bank Supervision Process" booklet of the Comptroller's Handbook provide guidance on communication with foreign supervisors. In accordance with PPM 5500-1, IB&F is responsible for coordinating, developing, and maintaining working relationships with foreign bank supervisory and regulatory authorities. Examiners having questions about any communication with foreign supervisors should consult district counsel.

The OCC must adapt policies and guidance governing national banks to the structural characteristics of federal branches and agencies. This section gives examiners an understanding of the basic legal framework of federal branches and agencies, information on important regulatory requirements, and succinct guidance on important areas of examination.

Capital Equivalency Deposits

In accordance with 12 USC 3102(g) and 12 CFR 28.15 and subject to OCC's discretion, federal branches and agencies are required to maintain CEDs to protect depositors, safeguard the public interest, and maintain a sound financial condition. The OCC views CEDs primarily as a limited source of good quality assets, which during a liquidation may be sold to pay off third-party claims. In individual cases, the OCC may also require, for prudential or supervisory reasons, that a federal branch hold CEDs greater than the minimum. CEDs are not a basis for calculating limits based upon capital. Any limit or restriction based on capital stock and surplus refers to the U.S. dollar equivalent of the capital stock and surplus of the FBO.

When opening a federal branch or agency in any state, a foreign bank must establish and maintain a deposit account with a member bank in that state of at least (1) 5 percent of the total liabilities of the federal branch or agency, including acceptances but excluding accrued expenses, amounts due, and other liabilities to offices, branches, and subsidiaries of the foreign bank or (2) the amount of capital that would be required of a national bank being organized at the same location, whichever is greater. In most instances, the minimum amount of the initial CED will be 5 percent of total liabilities.

CEDs may consist of investment securities eligible for investment by national banks; U.S.-dollar-denominated deposits payable in the United States; certificates of deposit payable in the United States and banker's acceptances, provided that in either case the issuer or the instrument is rated investment grade by an internationally recognized rating organization (12 CFR 28.15[a]); or other assets that the OCC may permit. Commercial paper is eligible if it is an investment security (12 CFR 1.2[e]). Such a security must be marketable (12

CFR 1.2[f]) and be rated investment grade or be the credit equivalent of a security rated investment grade (12 CFR 1.2[d] and 12 CFR 1.2[e]).

The depository bank must be located in the same state as the federal branch or agency, and it must be a member of the Federal Reserve System. A depository bank meets the definition of "located in the same state" if it is either headquartered or operates a branch in the state in which the federal branch or agency is located.

A CED agreement is entered into by the FBO, the depository bank, and the OCC. The agreement governs the operation of the account, sets certain conditions, and stipulates that the instruments are held for the benefit of the Comptroller of the Currency and cannot be released or diminished without the prior written authorization of the OCC. The FBO's head office staff collects the interest on the funds or securities deposited and is permitted by the agreement to exchange funds or securities dollar for dollar.

Federal branches and agencies must maintain a capital equivalency ledger showing the amount of liabilities requiring capital equivalency coverage for each business day. Federal branches and agencies must ensure that call report (FFIEC 002) definitions and generally accepted accounting principles are followed when determining the level of liabilities subject to CED coverage.

On the last business day of each month, the average daily CED balance is computed. If this calculation shows that an increase in the deposit is required, the addition must be made no later than the second business day of the following month. For FBOs having more than one federal branch or agency in a state, the required CED balance is determined on an aggregate basis for all such federal branches or agencies in the state. However, the CED agreement must cover all federal branches and agencies.

Federal branches and agencies should monitor their CED balances continually. Changes in liabilities because of the ongoing business of the federal branch or agency may result in additional deposit requirements. If securities comprise all or part of the CED, interest-rate swings may lower the market value of securities held, necessitating additions to the deposit. The CED account is valued at principal or market value, whichever is lower. Changes in the financial condition of an obligor may also result in the downgrading of a security in the CED account to non-investment grade. Under such circumstances, the security would have to be replaced with an investment that qualifies under 12 USC 24(7) and 12 CFR 28.15. Securities that are part of the CED account may be subject to Financial Accounting Standard 115, which addresses the accounting for investments in debt and equity securities.

Federal branch or agency management must maintain adequate documentation that will allow examiners to review compliance with 12 CFR 28.15 during examinations. The Comptroller's Corporate Manual for Federal Branches and Agencies includes procedures for the establishment and maintenance of CEDs, including account reductions and changes in depository banks.

Regulatory Reports

Federal branches and agencies file quarterly call reports completed on form FFIEC 002, "Report of Assets and Liabilities of U.S. Branches and Agencies of Foreign Banks." The report requests data on the entire operation of the federal branch or agency, including its international banking facility (segregated business conducted with foreign residents under strict restrictions), if applicable. However, income statement information is not included. Branches in the same state can file a consolidated report.

The federal branch or agency managers who are responsible for managing or controlling the assets and liabilities of a branch outside the United States must also file the call report supplement (FFIEC 002S). Under 12 CFR 28.11, a federal branch or agency "manages or controls" an offshore branch if it has most of the responsibility for business decisions, including decisions with regard to lending, asset management, funding, or liability management or if it is responsible for keeping the records of assets or liabilities for the offshore office. An offshore branch that is managed or controlled by a U.S. federal branch or agency may not engage in a type of activity that a U.S. bank could not manage at its branches or subsidiaries outside the United States.

Some federal branches and agencies may be required to file a country exposure report (Form FFIEC 019). The report is prepared quarterly "as of" the last business day of each calendar quarter. The report provides information on the distribution by country of claims on non-U.S. residents by U.S. branches and agencies of FBOs. The federal branch or agency must report its gross claims on (1) residents of its home country (including non-U.S. offices of the reporting institution) and (2) residents of the five other countries for which its adjusted exposure (i.e., direct claims adjusted for guarantees and other indirect claims) is largest, if the adjusted exposure for the country is also at least US$20 million.

Record Keeping

Each federal branch and agency must keep its accounts separate from those of the FBO and any other branch or agency. Accounts and records must be maintained in English to the extent necessary to permit OCC examiners to review the condition of the federal branch's or agency's and management's compliance with applicable laws (12 CFR 28.18(c)). When an FBO has more than one federal branch or agency in a state, head office management must also designate one of these offices to maintain consolidated asset, liability, and CED accounts for all federal branches and agencies in the state. Information requested from federal branch or agency management for use during the supervisory process should usually include only items carried on the books of the federal branch or agency and its international banking facility.

Operations Booked at Other FBO Offices

Federal branch or agency management will often conduct operations that, while managed at the federal branch or agency, are booked at another office of the FBO in the United States or offshore. For example, federal branch or agency management may generate or be responsible for loans, trading assets, deposits, or other business that are ultimately booked at, sold, or otherwise transferred to related offices. Adequate risk management processes, operational controls, and compliance programs covering all activities for which federal branch or agency management is effectively responsible should be in place. For example, if deposits are accepted at the federal branch on behalf of another FBO office, federal branch management should ensure compliance with BSA regulations, even if the deposits are immediately transferred to a non-U.S. office of the FBO.

The OCC does not have general supervisory authority over a foreign bank's offshore branches. Nevertheless, the OCC has concluded that it has the authority to examine the books of an FBO's offshore branch (provided they are available at the federal branch or agency), at least to the extent that the federal branch or agency manages the offshore branch's activities. The management or control of those offshore branch activities may be indicative of the quality of the management and policies of the federal branch or agency. The activities of the offshore branch may even have a direct effect on the condition and operations of the federal branch or agency. The OCC's authority to examine the books and records at an offshore branch outside the United States may depend on the laws of the host country. If a need arises in an examination of a federal branch or agency for documents at the offshore branch, and the federal branch or agency cannot produce the requested information, examiners should contact their district counsel for further guidance.

When the definition of "managed and controlled" is met, it is generally appropriate to evaluate the extent to which activities of the managed or controlled offshore branch may affect the condition of the federal branch or agency. Such evaluation would not address the condition of the offshore branch itself. Instead, it would detect any qualitative impact of the offshore branch's activities on the federal branch or agency. The scope of the evaluation would be limited to any activities of the offshore branch that the federal branch or agency manages. Examiners should assess how effective that management has been.

Since the assets of the offshore branch will generally consist of loans and interbank deposits, examiners may opt to perform a limited review of those portfolios and make a general but limited assessment of the asset quality in the offshore branch. The scope may include: a review of a sample of the offshore branch's asset portfolio for credit quality; an analysis of financial and other credit information, collateral, and documentation; and a general review of underwriting standards, policies and procedures, credit administration, internal audit, and credit review and evaluation processes.

In the report of examination, the examiner may choose to include general comments describing the quality of the federal branch's and agency's management of activities at the offshore branch. However, the offshore branch is not OCC's supervisory responsibility; therefore, it is important that the report of examination does not:

- Criticize as special mention or classify any assets booked at the offshore branch.

- Criticize as special mention or classify for credit risk the "due-from the offshore" account, even if a significant volume of criticized or classified assets are booked at the offshore branch. However, "due-from" accounts at the federal branch or agency (either from the head office or from the offshore branch or other branches outside the United States) may be reported as "other transfer risk problems" or classified for transfer risk, based on the Interagency Country Exposure Review Committee (ICERC) assessment of such risk.

- Schedule or describe totals of criticized or classified assets booked at the offshore branch.

- Direct any charge-offs, allowance for loan and lease losses, or allocated transfer risk reserve (ATRR) provisions for assets booked at the offshore branch.

- Include any other specific information regarding the offshore branch in the examination statistical data or in any other section of the report of examination.

- Cite activities that may be violations of law occurring at the offshore branch, unless such violations involve activities at the federal branch or agency that manages or controls the offshore branch.

Management and Supervision

Federal branches and agencies are normally run by an on-site general manager, the executive responsible for all decisions made at the federal branch or agency. Generally speaking, boards of directors of FBOs are not involved in the day-to-day supervision and administration of their federal branches or agencies. Such responsibility is usually delegated to head office senior management. Federal branch or agency management is held accountable for the effective implementation of adequate plans, policies, and controls. Therefore, as a practical matter, the OCC will ascribe the responsibility for establishing and maintaining adequate plans, policies and controls to federal branch or agency and head office senior management, rather than directly to the FBO board of directors. (In this booklet, "head office senior management" usually means officers who are directly responsible for supervising the federal branch or agency.)

There are no citizenship requirements for the person in charge of the federal branch or agency or for other personnel who work there. The general manager is usually an officer from the head office whose tenure at the federal branch or agency will normally last a few years. The FBO usually provides management continuity to the federal branch or agency; such continuity is not normally a significant supervisory concern.

Although the general manager is responsible for administering the affairs of the federal branch or agency, the FBO normally has considerable influence over which types of activities are conducted there. The extent of supervision and assistance provided by head office management should be evaluated during an examination. The adequacy of the federal branch or agency management's reporting to head office management should also be reviewed to ensure that head office management is aware of the overall condition and risks at the federal branch or agency.

Supervision by head office management takes many forms, including limiting permissible activities and setting the level of risk-taking. Other ways head office management assists the federal branch or agency include funding the CED and other deposits placed at the federal branch or agency, providing management expertise, helping it to obtain loans, performing audits and loan reviews, and developing policies and providing direction.

Asset Quality and Internal Loan Review

Examiners' evaluation of asset quality helps to assess the effectiveness of credit risk management. It also affords an accurate measure of problem assets. The evaluation takes on added importance when the FBO's ability to support it is increasingly in doubt and its involuntary liquidation seems likely.

Loans, investment securities, and money market assets are usually the primary earning assets at a federal branch or agency. Loans at federal branches and agencies are generally made to medium-sized and large corporate customers. The preponderance of federal branches and agencies participate in the loan syndication market and extend trade finance credit. When reviewing trade finance activities, examiners should seek guidance from the "Trade Finance" booklet of the Comptroller's Handbook. A few federal branches and agencies are also active in large commercial underwritings. Because it is often difficult for federal branches and agencies to establish a niche in the local domestic market, loans may be obtained through participation with correspondent banks or through the head office or other offices of the FBO. Foreign companies that have a presence in the United States and are from the same home country as the federal branch or agency are also usually a good source of business. U.S. companies conducting business in the FBO's home country are another source.

Core assessment procedures used to evaluate credit risk in national banks may be used in federal branches and agencies. However, examiners should judge the quality and quantity of credit risk at the federal branch or agency with an eye to its relationship with the FBO. Examiners should ensure that management has implemented an effective internal system to identify problem loans.

Although allocated transfer risk reserve requirements are not applicable to the cross-border exposures of federal branches and agencies, the ICERC transfer risk ratings do apply. If the federal branch or agency has exposure to a country that is rated "other transfer risk problems" or worse, examiners should provide management with the applicable ICERC country write-up. Examiners may also provide write-ups for countries that are rated weak or moderately strong if there are concerns about the level of the federal branch's or agency's exposure to the country.

Examiners evaluating asset quality in federal branch and agency examinations sometimes encounter loans or other assets that are booked at the federal branch or agency as an accommodation to the FBO's head office or one of its other offices inside or outside the United States. In general, while the asset is funded with federal branch or agency funds, the other office retains all other internal administrative and credit responsibilities within the FBO. The assets often lack credit, financial, or collateral documentation. Federal branch and agency managers usually say that they rely on the other office to maintain such supporting information and documentation. The federal branch or agency often has an explicit guarantee or repurchase agreement from the head office on these assets. Local management may assert that such arrangements preclude losses. However, it is OCC policy that all assets held by and booked at a federal branch or agency be adequately supported by credit and financial information, as well as collateral and other documentation. Even assets generated by other offices of the FBO should be so supported. This policy is similar to that on asset participation by national banks.

The existence of head office guarantees, standby letters of credit, or repurchase arrangements does not relieve federal branch or agency management of this documentation requirement. Presumably, the federal branch's or agency's FBO already implicitly assures the continuing overall viability of the federal branch or agency: it is responsible for the ongoing support of the federal branch's or agency's operations. From a supervisory perspective, the addition of such explicit guarantees, repurchase agreements, or other similar arrangements for specific assets does not add anything to the already-implied assurance of support. Therefore, the absence of supporting information should be criticized during examinations and corrective action required.

Loans in federal branches and agencies are subject to legal lending limits (12 USC 84). The calculation of the legal lending limit is based on the U.S. dollar equivalent of the FBO's capital. To determine compliance, the FBO must aggregate exposures at all federal branches and agencies with any state branch and agency exposures. To enable the OCC to monitor compliance, the FBO must designate one federal branch or agency office to maintain the consolidated information.

Federal branch and agency management may ask examiners to issue an express determination letter if the federal branch or agency has elected to use regulatory accounting in its tax accounting for bad debts. Examiners should obtain the concurrence of the FBO before issuing the letter. This step is appropriate as a means of assessing the level of FBO involvement and supervision in this area.

Federal branches and agencies can usually hold the same investment securities and money market assets as national banks pursuant to 12 USC 24(7). Therefore, all federal branches and agencies must comply with OCC's supervisory guidance on the prudent operation of securities activities. The guidance covers such subjects as reporting requirements, the risk management of financial derivatives, and internal controls. Examiners may be required to modify the core assessment procedures or optional specific banking activities procedures applicable to national banks.

Like the legal lending limit, investment limits are based on the FBO's capital accounts. Federal branch or agency management should seek the advice of their accounting firm on the booking of unrealized gains and losses in available-for-sale securities. Since federal branches and agencies do not have capital accounts, gains or losses will be applied to the due-from/due-to head office accounts. (Due-from account balances are the head office's borrowings from the federal branch; due-to balances are the federal branch's borrowings from the head office.)

Small Business Loans

The OCC and other federal bank and thrift supervisors issued a policy statement on the documentation of loans to small and medium-sized businesses and farms on March 30, 1993. That policy is intended to eliminate unnecessary documentation on small and medium-sized businesses and farm loans for institutions that are highly rated and adequately capitalized. These institutions are allowed to identify, within certain limits, an "exempt portion" of their small and medium-sized business and farm loan portfolios, which are evaluated solely on performance and exempt from examiner criticism of documentation inadequacies. Additional information on the program may be found in the "Commercial Loans" section of the Comptroller's Handbook.

Federal branches and agencies are permitted to pursue lending to these customers under the general guidelines detailed in the policy statement for domestic U.S. financial institutions. Such lending, when undertaken, should conform to clearly defined policies from the FBO approving this activity and delineating its scope. The size and scope of such lending should reflect the expertise of the FBO and its U.S. offices in lending to small and medium-sized businesses and farms in the United States.

A federal branch or agency is eligible for participation in the program if it was assigned a composite ROCA rating of 1 or 2 at its most recent examination, and the federal branch or agency, its FBO, or any other of the FBO's U.S. offices is not subject to an enforcement action originated by a federal or state bank supervisor.

Except in insured federal branches, the limits established in the March 30, 1993, policy statement are based on the FBO's consolidated total capital. For insured federal branches, the limits must be based on the excess of eligible assets over liabilities (12 CFR Ch. III, 346.20[a]) maintained at the individual federal branch. For each FBO, the limits established in the March 30, 1993, policy statement will apply to the aggregate of the loans granted pursuant to this policy by all U.S. branches and agencies of the FBO. Small and medium-sized business and farm loans eligible for the program will be limited to those extended to U.S. residents.

All other requirements and limits of the interagency policy statement will be applicable to the small and medium-sized business and farm lending of federal branches and agencies.

Concentrations of Credit

As part of the FBO, a federal branch or agency does not have a separate capital structure. Consequently, concentration risk in assets cannot be fully assessed at the federal branch or agency level. A high concentration within the federal branch or agency may be minuscule within the FBO as a whole.

To fully assess concentration, examiners would have to obtain additional information from the FBO. Because doing so would increase the reporting burden and duplicate home country supervision, the review should instead assess the systems and procedures at the federal branch or agency that enable head office management to adequately monitor and manage its risk arising from asset concentrations.

Allowance for Loan and Lease Losses

OCC policy requires national banks to maintain an allowance for loan and lease losses (ALLL) that is adequate to absorb estimated inherent losses. For the following reasons, a federal branch- or agency-specific ALLL is not required:

- The OCC recognizes that the FBO's financial support is essential to the viability of a federal branch or agency. Also helping to make branch-specific ALLL unnecessary is the FBO's maintenance of loan loss reserves on a consolidated basis. (A rule requiring an FBO to keep a branch-specific ALLL would favor national banks, which are not required to do so.)

- For a federal branch or agency, an ALLL is generally a memorandum account which may be segregated in the federal branch's or agency's due-from/due-to head office accounts balance. Requiring an ALLL to be booked at the federal branch or agency may not necessarily result in increased resources for the federal branch or agency, unless federal branch or agency management is also required to maintain a net due-to position with the head office and related parties.

- For FBOs in unsatisfactory condition or otherwise posing a higher-than-normal degree of risk, the OCC will closely monitor the federal branch's or agency's net due-from/due-to head office accounts and make use of asset maintenance requirements, which can more effectively foster the protection of third-party creditors.

Although an ALLL is not required, federal branches and agencies must meet ALLL-related documentation requirements (see the "Allowance for Loan and Lease Losses" booklet of the Comptroller's Handbook). Management must maintain adequate documentation to demonstrate the adequacy and effectiveness of its loan review and internal control systems. This documentation will help examiners assess the adequacy of the credit risk management process.

Federal branch or agency management may prefer to maintain a branch- or agency-specific ALLL. If so, it may base the amount of the ALLL on home country provisioning rules (generally because of tax considerations). When using that basis, federal branch or agency management must ensure that the method produces an adequate ALLL and that results are similar to those achieved by applying the guidelines in the "Allowance for Loan and Lease Losses" booklet of the Comptroller's Handbook.

Asset/Liability Management

Although the federal branch or agency constitutes only a portion of the FBO, examiners should evaluate balance sheet management. Management should establish appropriate written policies, short- and long-term strategic planning, and accurate reporting systems. Although written policies and procedures may be based on those of the FBO, they should be tailored to the federal branch's or agency's goals and objectives. (They should be approved by head office management.)

In order to evaluate the balance sheet management processes of a federal branch or agency, the examiner must develop an understanding of the customer mix, asset/liability composition, off-balance-sheet contingencies, offshore activities, the economic and competitive environment, and the management structure of the FBO.

The balance sheet of federal branches and agencies differs from that found at most national banks. Typically, the maturity of assets and liabilities is relatively short-term. Assets are often trade financings for medium-sized and large corporations, as well as money market investments. Funding is usually obtained from the wholesale funding markets and the FBO. Retail lending and deposit-taking are typically minimal.

In recent years, the composition and maturity structure of federal branch and agency balance sheets have changed in response to competitive pressures and globalization of financial markets. Federal branches and agencies are expanding from traditional business lines into such activities as real estate, mortgage-backed securities, high-yield securities, and structured notes.

Like other globally active banks, many federal branches and agencies are actively expanding their off-balance-sheet activities. These activities have traditionally included unfunded loan commitments, letters of credit, and spot and forward foreign exchange. Off-balance-sheet activities now commonly include active trading of derivative instruments such as swaps and option contracts. A federal branch or agency can trade for customers as well as its own account.

When evaluating balance sheet management, examiners should consider the organization's management structure. Depending on the head office's philosophy, management may be centralized or decentralized. In a centralized management system, risks (e.g., interest rate, price, and foreign exchange) arising from bank nontrading and trading portfolios are aggregated on a global basis and managed by the FBO. It is not unusual to find some FBOs controlling interest rate risks through a centralized internal funds transfer pricing system managed at the head office, usually the treasury unit. Under a decentralized system, federal branches or agencies are typically allocated risk sublimits (e.g., gap or earning-at-risk limits) and held responsible for managing within such sublimits. To control interest rate risks at the federal branch or agency, many FBOs also set "secondary" limits, including more traditional volume limits for maturities, coupons, markets, and instruments. The federal branch or agency should have operational controls that identify, quantify, and control the risk within that portfolio. Systems within the federal branch or agency should be sufficiently sophisticated to monitor and control all aspects of risks not managed by the head office. Depending on the specific risk management structure, criticism of rate sensitivity imbalances at the federal branch or agency may not be warranted if the exposure is hedged within the limits established by the FBO.

Federal branches or agencies may use derivatives to manage their interest rate, price, foreign exchange, and other risks arising from business activities. Supervisory guidance on the use of derivatives can be found in the "Risk Management of Financial Derivatives" booklet of the Comptroller's Handbook.

The FBO should develop projections for balance sheet growth in annual budgets of federal branches and agencies. Head office and federal branch and agency management should then monitor progress with periodic rate-variance and volume-variance reporting. Depending on the quality of borrowers (typically investment grade) and the cost of interest-bearing liabilities (usually higher due to the wholesale nature of funding), the spread generated by earning assets may be lower than that typically found in national banks.

Examiners should refer to the "Interest Rate Risk" and "Asset Securitization" booklets of the Comptroller's Handbook for more information on evaluating balance sheet management.

Liquidity

When evaluating liquidity, examiners should bear in mind that the federal branch or agency is part of the FBO. Examiners should gain an understanding of the FBO's current financial condition and any potential liquidity concerns that could affect the federal branch or agency. They should be aware that the federal branch's or agency's liquidity is influenced by the market perception of the FBO. If the FBO becomes troubled (but before continued viability becomes an issue), it may be appropriate to impose supervisory liquidity requirements on the federal branch or agency. Such requirements might include maintenance of a net due-to position and liquid assets.

Examiners will find that the overall level, nature, and significance of the federal branch's or agency's funding relationship with its FBO is influenced by several factors, including the FBO's financial condition, economic and market conditions in the home country, comparative funding costs in the home country versus the United States, the market perception of the FBO, and the branch's role, if any, in the overall funding strategy of the FBO's other U.S. operations. A primary source of funding for both insured and uninsured federal branches and agencies remains the wholesale market. Both insured and uninsured federal branches also rely on the FBO's head office and other offices for funding as a primary or secondary liquidity source. Funding from the head office and affiliates can be a source of low-cost or cost-free funds. The federal branch or agency management may act as agent for its FBO and sell the FBO's commercial paper, the proceeds of which may fund the operations of the federal branch or agency and the FBO. Because federal branches and agencies may depend on the FBO for primary and secondary liquidity, the FBO's borrowing capacity will affect the federal branch's or agency's liquidity level.

Insured federal branches in existence on the date of FDICIA's enactment have an additional source of funding in the form of retail customer deposits. These grandfathered federal branches are empowered to accept deposits of less than $100,000. Uninsured federal branches cannot accept deposits of less than $100,000 unless the deposit is exempted by 12 CFR 28.16. Therefore, an uninsured federal branch's funding sources are the head office and affiliates, Eurodollar and federal funds markets, and wholesale deposits. (Federal agencies are prohibited from accepting deposits.)

Funding volatility should be analyzed using appropriate examination procedures. (As always, examiners should recognize that a federal branch or agency cannot be analyzed as a stand-alone unit.) If any liquidity concerns are identified, the examiner should conduct a more in-depth evaluation of the federal branch's or agency's liquidity. This evaluation should consider the federal branch's or agency's funds management profile with close attention to funding sources, funding gaps, funds management policy guidance from the head office, current economic and market conditions, and the adequacy of the contingency funding plan.

A major factor to consider in evaluating liquidity is whether the FBO has been a consistent supplier of funds, or whether the federal branch or agency acts as a dollar-funding vehicle for the FBO. The examiner should determine whether the federal branch or agency serves as a net user or net provider of funds for the FBO. The analysis, which is particularly important if the FBO raises liquidity concerns, is described in the "Due-From/To Head Office Account" section of this booklet.

Federal branch and agency management should be guided and supported by appropriate written policies, short- and long-term planning, and accurate reporting systems. Written policies and procedures should be approved by the head office's senior management and reflect the federal branch's or agency's role in the FBO's global strategy.

Trading Activities

Trading activities are becoming a growing and significant source of revenue for federal branches and agencies. To offer competitive products to their customers and generate additional revenue, federal branches and agencies have increased both the volume of their trading activities and the complexity of the financial instruments traded. While historically active in spot and forward foreign exchange trading, federal branches and agencies are now active in trading fixed income securities, emerging market debt, and derivative instruments such as swaps, options, and structured notes.

In recent years, there have been some widely reported trading losses experienced at overseas branches of globally active financial institutions and corporations. Contributing to the trading losses were inadequate senior management oversight, excessive risk-taking, insufficient understanding of the instruments traded, poor internal controls, and lack of an independent revaluation process. Because federal branches and agencies can be thousands of miles and several time zones from their FBO, strong reporting, risk management, and internal control systems are particularly important to ensure the proper oversight of their activities.

Trading activities involve price, credit, liquidity, transaction, compliance, reputation, and strategic risks. Because the risk management guidelines in the

"Risk Management of Financial Derivatives" and "Emerging Market Country Products and Trading Activities" booklets of the Comptroller's Handbook apply to the trading of various types of financial instruments, they should be consulted when examiners review federal branch and agency trading activities.

Most of the risk produced by the federal branch's or agency's trading activities may be managed at the FBO. Federal branch or agency management may have little control over the FBO's risk management systems. However, in general, a federal branch's or agency's systems for controlling trading risk should be as sophisticated as those of a national bank conducting similar activities. In particular, examiners should ensure that head office management has established at the federal branch or agency: policy and limits governing trading activities; internal control systems; independent risk management mechanisms to monitor risk levels and test adherence to policy and risk limits; and an accurate and timely reporting process. Strong controls should ensure that trading instruments are revalued independently of the risk-taker.

When the federal branch's or agency's risk management systems do not comply with OCC risk management guidelines, examiners should obtain commitments from federal branch or agency management to rectify deficiencies. These issues should be documented in the work papers and the ROE, and they should receive appropriate follow-up.

Earnings

Federal branch or agency earnings are evaluated in relation to the FBO's mission and objectives in establishing a U.S. presence and the role of the federal branch or agency within the FBO. Therefore, earnings should be evaluated against budgeted projections, as well as for the integrity of the reported results.

A comparison of period-to-period performance may be conducted to determine trends. Consideration should be given to the following: the quality and composition of earnings, the strength of the net interest margin, and the vulnerability of earnings to market and interest rate changes. The reliance on unusual or nonrecurring gains or losses, the contribution of extraordinary items, the effect of securities or other trading activities, and plans for enhancing earnings or correcting earnings deficiencies are also considerations.

For an earnings analysis of a federal branch or agency to be complete, the FBO's overall U.S. operation may have to be considered. For example, a low spread at the federal branch or agency could be caused by the FBO's competitive strategy or market standing. Or the federal branch or agency may have the unprofitable part of a lending and deposit relationship that is profitable for the FBO as a whole.

Internal Controls and Audit

In principle, methods of evaluating internal controls and the audit function in a national bank also apply in a federal branch or agency. Accordingly, the "Internal Control" booklet of the Comptroller's Handbook may be used. The operational areas may include lending, investments and funds management, and foreign exchange bookkeeping.

The audit function may consist of a combination of an internal audit, an inspection by the head office, and an external audit by an accounting firm. Examiners should determine whether audit reports are adequate. They should also determine whether federal branch or agency management's actions to correct identified deficiencies are adequate.

Insured federal branches with claims on non-related parties of $500 million or more are subject to the FDIC rule implementing the requirements of the FDIC Improvement Act of 1991. These insured federal branches should report their claims on non-related parties on their FFIEC 002 reports. The FDIC rule requires that independent accountants perform annual audits, conduct a separate examination, and report on the effectiveness of internal controls over reporting. Because insured federal branches do not have separate boards of directors, the audit committee requirements of the rule are not applied. Nonetheless, head office and local management of such federal branches should make a good faith effort to ensure compliance with the rule's requirements.

Private Banking

Although there is not a standard definition of private banking, most bankers would agree that private banking is targeted to persons of high net worth and their business interests. In private banking, a bank sells products through a single employee (private banker or relationship manager) rather than through the bank's different units.

Banks may offer private banking services through their trust departments, asset management division, private banking departments, or global affiliates (including affiliates in offshore banking centers). The services offered may include asset management relationships (such as trust, investment advice, and investment management accounts), custodial services, offshore facilities, funds transfer, foreign exchange trading, lending, and deposit account relationships. Because of the cross-functional nature of the services offered and the diversity of products, the private banker must be experienced and well-trained to comply with all the regulatory requirements in each area. The anti-money-laundering laws and regulations place significant compliance responsibilities on financial institutions. Using the "Bank Secrecy Act" booklet of the Comptroller's Handbook, the OCC conducts examinations of federal branches and agencies and tests for compliance with BSA regulations and other money-laundering laws.

Private banking may pose a high risk to the federal branch or agency because of its susceptibility to internal control exceptions. And because large amounts of money are managed through confidential relationships, the potential is there for money laundering.

In reviewing a federal branch's or agency's private banking activities, it is important to determine the adequacy of policies and procedures, internal controls, and auditing. Internal controls and independent audits are especially important because of the way private banking is conducted: the limited staffing in private banking departments makes it difficult to segregate duties, and the private banking customer may delegate a significant amount of decision-making authority to the private banker. Because these circumstances expose private banking accounts to possible manipulation, the federal branch or agency must have a process in place to identify suspicious activities and to report suspicious transactions in accordance with regulatory requirements. Bank anti-money-laundering and BSA compliance programs should cover private banking relationships and be reviewed by the audit program.

Much private banking involves providing deposit services to international customers. Sometimes these services are offered to customers in the form of accounts that protect their identity. A federal branch that provides deposit services must have adequate documentation to demonstrate that it is complying with the BSA, financial record-keeping, and reporting rules. The private banker must also comply with the financial record-keeping regulations and product suitability rules associated with securities activities. Depending on the arrangement with the customer, fiduciary regulations may also apply. When acting as a fiduciary, banks may have statutory, contractual, or ethical obligations to protect customer confidentiality.

Private banking clients often receive "hold mail service," which enables them to have bank statements and other documents held at the federal branch rather than mailed to their home or business. This service may be used by customers who need security or who live in countries where the mail service is unreliable. Since the customer does not review statements regularly, the risk is high that input errors and fraudulent or unauthorized transactions will not be detected quickly. An independent unit of the federal branch should periodically review hold-all-mail accounts, as well as dormant and inactive accounts.

An account may be opened in the name of an individual, a law firm, a business, or a private investment company (PIC). PICs are separate legal entities structured to hold a customer's personal assets. A PIC may also be an asset of a trust. A PIC may conduct transactions for its investors through its account at the federal branch.

The account agreement should fully document how the account works: it should specify to what extent decision making has been delegated to the private banker and what documentation is required from the customer to enable the private banker to execute transactions. Because each account holder can grant subaccount holders access to the private banking relationship, the agreement should also document who has access to the account, as well as the policies and procedures for granting this access. Accounts should not establish relationships with anonymous parties.

In examining the private banking function, the examiner may have to draw from various booklets of the Comptroller's Handbook to cover securities activities, lending, and fiduciary issues. Examiners may also review management information systems, identify and aggregate customer account information, and produce the reports required to monitor account activity. A review of the adequacy of the compliance and internal audit function will also be important. Examiners should review the "Bank Secrecy Act" booklet of the Comptroller's Handbook for more detailed procedures concerning money-laundering controls, identifying money laundering, and promoting compliance with BSA regulations and other money-laundering laws.

Due-From/To Head Office Account

The due-from head office account balance represents loans or placements, including clearing balances, extended by the federal branch or agency to its head office or to other related offices. Due-to account balances represent borrowing by the federal branch or agency from its head office or other related offices. The net due-to position is one indication of the FBO's financial support for the federal branch or agency; this balance may fund the CED, ongoing and expanding operations, and the ALLL, if any, and it is available to cover third-party obligations as necessary.

The due-from head office account often funds export financing from the home country. In such arrangements, payments from the head office account are often scheduled to come from the receiving party. Unless the underlying trade documents are held at the federal branch or agency and the receiving party (importer) is obligated to pay the federal branch or agency, the transaction poses transfer risk. Often, the receiving party pays the head office and the head office repays the federal branch or agency.

Any time the repayment for an asset comes from a foreign country, the transaction poses transfer risk. Transfer risk is the possibility that an asset cannot be serviced in the currency of payment because of a lack of, or restraints on the availability of, foreign exchange in the obligor's country. In the case of head office accounts, an FBO reversing a net due-from position could find it difficult to obtain dollars.

Credit risk in this context may be thought of as the FBO's inability to reverse the net due-from position because of solvency or liquidity problems. Therefore, the amount of credit risk posed by a net due-from position is directly proportionate to the strength of support provided by the FBO. But the size of the net due-from position is only an indicator and not one of the primary determinants of the amount of credit risk. Although a net due-from position equal to more than 50 percent of the federal branch's or agency's total assets may suggest high credit risk, the risk may be relatively low. Large net due-from positions on financially strong FBOs operating in stable markets may pose less risks than small net due-from positions on weak FBOs in unstable economies.

If a federal branch has a net due-from head office position, it may not be able to pay off third-party liabilities in the course of its regular business or in the event of liquidation. The appropriateness of a federal branch's or agency's net due-from (or net due-to) position should be determined case by case using at least the following considerations: (1) the strength of support provided by the FBO (the strength of support assessment evaluates the FBO's overall financial condition, including its liquidity; its managerial and operational record; the system of supervision in its home country; the economic environment and financial system in which it operates; and other pertinent factors, including a judgment on the FBO's ability to maintain adequate internal controls and compliance procedures at its U.S. offices); (2) the FBO's strategies for funding the federal branch or agency and their consistency with U.S. business plans; (3) a review of policies governing financial transactions with the head office and other related offices; and (4) the federal branch's or agency's liquidity position.

Compliance

The activities of federal branches and agencies are generally subject to the same compliance requirements as national banks. Head office management should ensure that adequate systems and controls are in place at the federal branch or agency to comply with U.S. laws and OCC's supervisory requirements. Head office management must ensure that the federal branch or agency has a competent and independent compliance function whose staff is properly trained and informed about pertinent U.S. laws and regulations.

Federal branches and agencies do not always engage in the same activities as national banks and, therefore, are not always subject to the same laws and regulations as national banks. For instance, the Community Reinvestment Act does not generally apply to federal agencies or uninsured federal branches. And consumer laws may have only limited application for the many federal branches that do not engage in consumer lending.

Using their knowledge of the activities of individual federal branches and agencies, examiners should decide which compliance procedures, if any, need to be applied. When performing compliance procedures, examiners should follow the procedures in the Comptroller's Handbook for Compliance and the Comptroller's Handbook. Supervisory strategies should include compliance examination activities applicable to the business of the federal branch or agency.

Core Assessment

Explanation

Examiners should review the supervision by risk discussion in this booklet's introduction when evaluating the core assessment factors below. The conclusions reached in the core assessment can provide greater support for the conclusions reached on overall and individual ROCA components. The core assessment and the ROCA evaluation should be as consistent as possible. Examiners should recognize that the FBO may rapidly and substantially alter the risk profile of the federal branch or agency; therefore, the risk profile of the federal branch or agency should also be viewed in the context of the overall strength of support the FBO may be able to provide.

The large bank core assessment standards have been tailored for federal branches and agencies. Assessments should be updated during every examination cycle for federal branches or agencies.

Credit Risk

Quantity of Credit Risk

Examiners should consider the following assessment factors when making judgments about the quantity of credit risk. These factors are the minimum standards that all examiners will consider when completing the risk assessment (appendix B). Examiners should apply the standards consistent with the guidelines in the "Loan Portfolio Management" booklet of the Comptroller's Handbook. These factors are consistent with the framework for the ongoing supervisory approach used in large banks. At a minimum, they should be reviewed, monitored, and analyzed during every supervisory cycle (every 12 months or 18 months) to ensure quality supervision. Using the core assessment factors, examiners assess whether the risk is low, moderate, or high.

Low   Moderate   High

Underwriting Factors   •   •   •

- Changes in underwriting standards including leverage, policies, price, tenor, collateral, guarantor support, covenants, and structure.
- The borrower's ability to service debt based on debt service coverage, debt/income ratios, and credit history.
- The volume and extent of exceptions.

                                Low   Moderate   High

Strategic Factors   •   •   •

- The impact of strategic factors including the target market, the portfolio and product mix, acquisitions, diversification of repayment sources, new products, third-party originations, and concentrations.
- The maintenance of an appropriate balance between risk and reward.

                                Low   Moderate   High

External Factors   •   •   •

- The impact of external factors including economic, industry, competitive, and market conditions; legislative and regulatory changes; and technological advancement.
- Recent or anticipated changes in the FBO's strategy that may substantially alter the risk profile of the federal branch or agency.

                                Low   Moderate   High

Credit Quality Factors   •   •   •

- The levels and trends of delinquencies, nonperforming and problem assets, losses, weighted average risk ratings, and reserves.
- Trends in the growth and volume of lending and fee-based credit activities, including off-balance-sheet, investment, payment, settlement, and clearing activities.
- Trends in the financial performance of borrowers and counterparties.
- Trends identified in loan pricing methods, portfolio analytics, loss forecasting, and stress testing methods.
- Trends in summary ratings assigned by loan review and audit.

Quality of Credit Risk Management

Examiners should consider the following assessment factors when making judgments about the quality of credit risk management. These factors are the minimum standards that all examiners will consider when completing a risk assessment. Examiners should apply the standards consistent with the guidelines in the "Loan Portfolio Management" booklet of the Comptroller's Handbook. These factors are consistent with the framework for the ongoing supervisory approach used in large banks. At a minimum, they should be reviewed, monitored, and analyzed during the course of a supervisory cycle (every 12 or 18 months) to ensure quality supervision. Using the core assessment factors, examiners assess whether the risk management is strong, satisfactory, or weak.

	Strong	Satisfactory	Weak
Policies	•	•	•

- The consistency of the federal branch's or agency's credit policy with the FBO's overall strategic direction and tolerance limits outlined for the federal branch or agency.
- The appropriate balance of the credit culture between credit and marketing.
- The structure of the credit operation and whether responsibility and accountability are assigned at every level.
- The reasonableness of definitions that determine policy, underwriting, and documentation exceptions.
- The appropriateness of credit guidelines that establish risk limits or positions and whether periodic revaluation is required.
- The approval of the federal branch's or agency's credit policy by head office management.

	Strong	Satisfactory	Weak
Processes	•	•	•

- The adequacy of processes that communicate policies and expectations to personnel.
- The production of timely and useful management information.
- The adequacy of processes to approve and monitor compliance with policy limits.
- The quality of processes to control the accuracy, completeness, and integrity of data.

- The adequacy of internal controls including segregation of duties, dual controls, etc.

Credit Granting
- The appropriateness of the approval process, marketing campaigns, and delivery channels.
- The thoroughness of the underwriting analysis, including a sensitivity analysis of borrower projections.
- The sufficiency of the method used to analyze the creditworthiness of counterparties and debt issuers to ensure repayment capacity, lien perfection, collateral valuation, and on-site inspection of collateral.
- The quality of analytical resources, such as portfolio models, and the adequacy of their periodic revalidation.

Credit Monitoring
- The adequacy of portfolio management, including the ability to identify and monitor risk relating to credit structure and concentrations.
- The adequacy of portfolio stress testing and restoring.
- The adequacy of credit analysis, including financial assessment and comparison of projections to actual performance.
- The frequency and reliability of verifying compliance with covenants.
- The accuracy and integrity of internal risk-rating processes.

Collection Efforts
- The development and execution of action plans and collection strategies to facilitate timely collection.
- The timely involvement of a specialized collection unit.

ALLL & Accounting Controls
- If a federal branch- or agency-specific ALLL is maintained because of home country provisioning rules, the results are similar to those achieved by applying the guidelines in the "Allowance for Loan and Lease Losses" booklet of the Comptroller's Handbook.
- Compliance with regulatory and accounting guidelines.

	Strong	Satisfactory	Weak
Personnel	•	•	•

- The extent of technical and managerial expertise.

- The appropriateness of performance management and compensation programs.
- The level of turnover of critical staff.
- The adequacy of training.

	Strong	Satisfactory	Weak
Control Systems	•	•	•

- The effectiveness and independence of the risk review, quality assurance, and audit functions.
- The accuracy, completeness, and integrity of management information systems and reports.
- The quality of exception monitoring systems that identify and measure incremental risk assumed by deviations from credit policy, established limits, and underwriting standards.
- The responsiveness of control systems to identified internal deficiencies in policy, process, and personnel.
- The responsiveness to identified deficiencies in internal controls.

Interest Rate Risk

Quantity of Interest Rate Risk

Examiners should consider the following assessment factors when making judgments about the quantity of interest rate risk. However, examiners should exercise judgment on the applicability of these assessment factors when the federal branch's or agency's interest rate risk is centrally managed at the head office. Under such circumstances, examiners should also pursue an understanding of the head office's global model for interest rate risk. These factors are the minimum standards that all examiners will consider when completing a risk assessment (appendix B). They are consistent with the framework for the ongoing supervisory approach used in large banks. At a minimum, they should be reviewed, monitored, and analyzed during the course of a supervisory cycle (every 12 or 18 months) to ensure quality supervision. Using the core assessment factors, examiners assess whether the risk is low, moderate, or high.

	Low	Moderate	High
Repricing Risk	•	•	•

- The repricing mismatch of assets and liabilities over the short- and long-term horizon.
- The adequacy of repricing distribution assumptions for nonmaturity deposit balances.
- The vulnerability of earnings to large interest rate changes, such as rate shocks and gradual rate shifts, e.g., a change of 200 basis points over 12 months.
- The presence of over-the-counter and exchange-traded derivatives, such as futures and interest rate swaps, used for rebalancing repricing mismatches.

	Low	Moderate	High
Basis Risk	•	•	•

- The use of different indexes to price assets and liabilities (e.g., prime, CMT, Libor, and 11th District COFI) that may change at different times or by different amounts.
- The presence of lagged or asymmetric pricing behavior on federal branch- or agency-managed rates such as consumer deposits.

- The impact of changes in cash flow and repricing correlations between hedging instruments and the positions being hedged.

	Low	Moderate	High
Yield Curve Risk	•	•	•

- The exposure of on- and off-balance-sheet positions to changes in the yield curve's absolute level and shape (e.g., rising level with flattening slope, falling level with steepening slope, curve inverts, and twists).

	Low	Moderate	High
Options Risk	•	•	•

- The extent of written (sold) options embedded in assets (e.g., loan and mortgage prepayments, interest rate caps and floors embedded in adjustable rate loans, and callable securities).
- The potential impact of written options embedded in liabilities (e.g., early deposit withdrawals, nonmaturity deposit elasticities, and callable liabilities).
- The volume of over-the-counter and exchange-traded options contracts.

	Low	Moderate	High
Strategic Factors	•	•	•

- The ability of the funding strategy to tolerate adverse interest rate movements.
- The impact of the federal branch's or agency's overall business strategy on interest rate risk (e.g., entering into new business activities or speculating on the direction and volatility of interest rates).

	Low	Moderate	High
External Factors	•	•	•

- The ability to withstand changes in interest rates caused by external factors including economic conditions, industry conditions, legislative and regulatory changes, market demographics, technological changes, competition, and market conditions.

Quality of Interest Rate Risk Management

Examiners should consider the following assessment factors when making judgments about the quality of interest rate risk management. These factors are the minimum standards that all examiners will consider when completing a risk assessment. These factors are consistent with the framework for the ongoing supervisory approach used in large banks. At a minimum, they should be reviewed, monitored, and analyzed during the course of a supervisory cycle (every 12 or 18 months) to ensure quality supervision. Using the core assessment factors, examiners assess whether the risk management is strong, satisfactory, or weak.

	Strong	Satisfactory	Weak
Policies	•	•	•

- The consistency of the federal branch's or agency's interest rate risk policy with the FBO's overall strategic direction and tolerance limits outlined for the federal branch or agency.
- The structure of the interest rate risk management function and whether responsibility and accountability are assigned at every level.
- The appropriateness of guidelines that establish risk limits or positions, including guidelines on how often they should be reassessed.
- The reasonableness of the definitions that determine policy exceptions and guidelines for approving policy exceptions.
- The approval of the federal branch's or agency's interest rate risk policy by head office management.
- The adequacy of the resources devoted to managing interest rate risk.

	Strong	Satisfactory	Weak
Processes	•	•	•

- The adequacy of processes communicating policies and expectations to appropriate personnel.
- The effectiveness of the process to reliably provide timely, accurate, and complete management information.
- The sufficiency of monitoring compliance with policy limits.
- The appropriateness of the approval process for policy exceptions.
- The appropriateness of risk measurement systems for the nature and complexity of activities, and how these systems are incorporated into the decision-making process.
- The ability of risk measurement systems to capture material positions and the risks inherent in the positions.

- The extent of clearly defined and reasonable measurement assumptions.
- The quality of processes to control the accuracy, completeness and integrity of data.
- The sufficiency of periodic stress tests that use scenarios reducing or eliminating profits and the tests' capacity to project accurately the effect of certain conditions.
- The vulnerability to limitations or weaknesses of measurement tools is understood.
- The ability of the risk measurement process to measure risk to earnings.
- The extent of consideration given to the impact of changing rates on noninterest income and expenses.
- The flexibility to modify positions in adverse rate environments in a timely manner.
- The reasonableness of responses to changes in market conditions.
- The adequacy of internal controls including separation of duties, dual controls, etc.

	Strong	Satisfactory	Weak
Personnel	•	•	•

- The extent of technical and managerial expertise.
- The appropriateness of performance management and compensation programs.
- The level of turnover of critical staff.
- The adequacy of training.

	Strong	Satisfactory	Weak
Control Systems	•	•	•

- The effectiveness of management information systems, reports, monitoring, and control functions.
- The independence of risk-monitoring and control functions from the risk-taking functions.
- The independence and validation of models and other measurement tools.
- The existence of systems that test the reasonableness and the validity of assumptions.
- The effectiveness of monitoring systems that track policy and limit exceptions, incremental risk exposure from exceptions, and corrective actions.
- The responsiveness of control systems to identify and respond to internal control deficiencies.

- The existence of an independent and competent audit function that validates the reliability and effectiveness of models and management processes.
- The responsiveness of control systems to identified deficiencies in policy, process, and personnel.

Liquidity Risk

Quantity of Liquidity Risk

Examiners should consider the following assessment factors when making judgments about the quantity of liquidity risk. These factors are the minimum standards that all examiners will consider when completing a risk assessment (appendix B). They are the framework for the ongoing supervisory approach used in large banks. At a minimum, they should be reviewed, monitored, and analyzed during the course of a supervisory cycle (every 12 or 18 months) to ensure quality supervision. Examiners should factor into their assessment any changes in the home country banking system's liquidity as well as the FBO's ability to provide financial support to the federal branch or agency if needed. The examiner should gain an understanding of the FBO's current financial condition and any potential liquidity concerns that could affect the federal branch or agency. Using the core assessment factors, examiners assess whether the risk is low, moderate, or high.

	Low	Moderate	High
Wholesale Liabilities	•	•	•

- The volume, composition, growth trends, and projections.
- The level of credit sensitivity.
- The level of customer loyalty generated through direct relationship management.
- The tenor, rates paid, collateralization requirements, and use of brokered deposits (greater than $100,000).

	Low	Moderate	High
Retail Liabilities	•	•	•

- The volume, composition, growth trends, and projections.
- The deposit mix and tenor.
- The loyalty and stability of the customer base.
- The use of brokered deposits (of $100,000 or less).

	Low	Moderate	High
Diversification	•	•	•

- The extent to which liabilities are diversified by individual funds provider, product, tenor, market area, industry, etc.
- The sufficiency of diversity by marketer, e.g., individual broker or direct placement.
- The appropriateness of investment objectives or economic influences.
- The extent of asset diversification as evidenced by the variety of loans and investments or other assets that could be used to raise funds.

	Low	Moderate	High
On- and Off-balance-sheet Cash Flows	•	•	•

- The capacity of the federal branch or agency and the FBO to access additional unsecured market funding.
  - In the current environment.
  - In a distressed environment.
- The existence of current and projected securitization activities, either as a source or potential use of funds including:
  - The extent of reliance on cash flows from securitization activities (i.e., is securitization used occasionally to enhance liquidity or is it "pipeline" financing required for ongoing business?).
  - Compliance with covenants.
  - The potential for early amortization (use of funds).
- The presence of other off-balance-sheet items which could result in cash flows to or from the balance sheet including:
  - Unused loan commitments.
  - Letters of credit or other contingent liabilities.
  - Collateral requirement agreements.
  - Early liability termination arrangements.
  - Calls, options.
- Size of the net due-from head office account in relation to the home country economic environment and financial condition of the FBO.

	Low	Moderate	High
Net Funding Gaps	•	•	•

- The volume of on- and off-balance-sheet net funding gaps.
- The extent of short- and long-term cash flow gaps in the existing structure.

- The projected growth or depletion of assets and liabilities.
- The extent of dependence on credit-sensitive sources.
- The adequacy of current and projected cash flow projections in normal environments (i.e., day-to-day activities), as well as in significantly deteriorated environments (usually best demonstrated in the contingency funding plan).
- The ability to cover projected funding gaps when needed in a cost-effective manner.

	Low	Moderate	High
External and Environmental Factors	•	•	•

- How the market views the FBO's:
  — Asset quality, earnings, and capital.
  — Reputation risk or other credit-related characteristics that could influence customer behavior.
- If available, the impact of the FBO and affiliates' current and projected:
  — Asset quality, earnings, and capital.
  — Liquidity, especially relating to commercial paper coverage.
  — Reputation risk or other characteristics that could influence customer behavior.
- The impact of the external market environment on the FBO (and the consequential impact on its federal branches or agencies), including:
  — Rating agency ratings and trends.
  — Relative cost of funds (debt spreads over comparable U.S. Treasury securities, compared with those of competitors).
  — Economic conditions, including job growth, migration, industry concentrations, competition, etc.

	Low	Moderate	High
Liquid Asset-based Factors	•	•	•

- The relationship of volume and trends in liquid assets compared with volume and trends of liabilities.
- The volume and composition of money market assets such as fed funds sold, Eurodollars placed, and certificates of deposit (CDs) purchased.
- The volume and composition of free securities (e.g., securities unencumbered by pledging and repurchase agreements).
- The amount of depreciation in the free securities holdings.
- The appropriateness of the unit size of free securities to provide for effective utilization.

- The capacity to enhance liquidity through asset sales or securitization.
- The federal branch's or agency's experience in asset sales or securitization markets.

Quality of Liquidity Risk Management

Examiners should consider the following assessment factors when making judgments about the quality of liquidity management. These factors are the minimum standards that all examiners will consider when completing a risk assessment. These factors are consistent with the framework for the ongoing supervisory approach used in large banks. At a minimum, they should be reviewed, monitored, and analyzed during the course of a supervisory cycle (every 12 or 18 months) to ensure quality supervision. Using the core assessment factors, examiners assess whether the risk management is strong, satisfactory, or weak.

	Strong	Satisfactory	Weak
Policies	•	•	•

- The appropriateness of stated limits.
- The appropriateness of guidelines for diversification and concentrations.
- Whether the policy establishes appropriate responsibilities and accountability.
- The periodic approval of the federal branch's or agency's liquidity policy by head office management.

	Strong	Satisfactory	Weak
Processes	•	•	•

- The adequacy of the financial planning and management strategy.
- Whether policies and expectations are communicated to appropriate personnel.
- The depth of contingency funding planning.
- The appropriateness of management oversight and responsiveness.
- The adherence to, and reporting of, limit compliance.
- The adequacy of internal controls including segregation of duties, dual controls, etc.

	Strong	Satisfactory	Weak
Personnel	•	•	•

- The extent of technical and managerial expertise.
- The appropriateness of the performance management and compensation programs.
- The level of turnover of critical staff.
- The adequacy of training.

	Strong	Satisfactory	Weak
Control Systems	•	•	•

- The timeliness, accuracy, and comprehensiveness of management information systems.
- The appropriateness of the distribution of management information systems reports.
- The appropriateness of limits governing balance sheet composition (ratios), cash flow (funding gaps), diversification (concentrations), and the amount provided by any one source of funds.
- The adequacy of the process for approval, monitoring, and reporting of limits.
- The adequacy of assumptions, scenario definitions, communication channels, and crisis management capabilities within the contingency funding plan.
- The timeliness and adequacy of reports to head office management.
- The adequacy of internal/external audit.
- The responsiveness to internal control deficiencies.
- The responsiveness of control systems to identified deficiencies in policy, process, and personnel.

Price Risk

Quantity of Price Risk

Examiners should consider the following assessment factors when making judgments about the quantity of price risk. These factors are the minimum standards that all examiners will consider when completing a risk assessment (appendix B). These factors are consistent with the framework for the ongoing supervisory approach used in large banks. At a minimum, they should be reviewed, monitored, and analyzed during the course of a supervisory cycle (every 12 or 18 months) to ensure quality supervision. Using the core assessment factors, examiners assess whether the risk is low, moderate, or high.

	Low	Moderate	High
Volume of Open Positions	•	•	•

- The level of open positions expressed as earnings at risk.
- The size of illiquid positions.

	Low	Moderate	High
Market Factors	•	•	•

- The price sensitivity to various market factors (e.g., foreign exchange, interest rates, equity, or commodity prices) in portfolios without options (linear portfolios).

	Low	Moderate	High
Options Risk	•	•	•

- The existence of nonlinear price sensitivity to changes in market factors.

- The existence of discontinuous option exposure (e.g., the exposure arising from path-dependent options).

	Low	Moderate	High
Basis Risk	•	•	•

- The volume of potential exposure caused by a change in the correlation between two prices (e.g., when the price of a derivative instrument and the price of an asset it is hedging do not move in tandem).

	Low	Moderate	High
Concentration of Factors	•	•	•

- The level and diversification among products or types of products.
- The existence of concentrations in market factors (e.g., option strike prices).

	Low	Moderate	High
Product Liquidity	•	•	•

- The volume of readily marketable products that generally can be liquidated or hedged within a reasonable time frame.
- The volume of illiquid products whose prices may decline because managers need a relatively long time to liquidate or effectively hedge them.

	Low	Moderate	High
Stability of Trading Revenue	•	•	•

- Revenue derived from customer-initiated trades in proportion to revenue derived from proprietary trading activity.

Quality of Price Risk Management

Examiners should consider the following assessment factors when making judgments about the quality of price risk management. These factors are the minimum standards that all examiners will consider when completing a risk assessment. These factors are consistent with the framework for the ongoing supervisory approach used in large banks. At a minimum, they should be reviewed, monitored, and analyzed during the course of a supervisory cycle (every 12 or 18 months) to ensure quality supervision. Using the core assessment factors, examiners assess whether the risk management is strong, satisfactory, or weak.

	Strong	Satisfactory	Weak
Policies	•	•	•

- The consistency of the federal branch's or agency's price risk policy with the FBO's overall strategic direction and tolerance limits outlined for the federal branch or agency.
- Risk-taking is clearly defined, and the risk-taking function assigns responsibility and accountability at every level.
- The price risk guidelines establish limits or positions and call for periodic revaluation.
- The approval of the price risk policy by head office management.
- The existence of adequate standards for independent model validation, given the federal branch's or agency's price risk.

	Strong	Satisfactory	Weak
Processes	•	•	•

- The amount of oversight provided by management, the federal branch's or agency's as well as the head office's.
- The comprehensiveness of the strategic planning process.
- The adequacy of process controls over new product development.
- The processing capabilities of the front and back office systems, considering the current and projected size and scope of the trading operation.
- The appropriateness of trading management oversight (e.g., approving and monitoring compliance with limits, communicating policies and expectations to appropriate personnel).
- The adequacy of independent measurement and analysis of risk under a variety of scenarios, including stress tests.
- The adequacy of the models used for testing revenue vulnerability under probable and stress test scenarios.
- The adequacy of the internal controls for trading operations (front and back office) including segregation of duties, dual controls, etc.

	Strong	Satisfactory	Weak
Personnel	•	•	•

- The extent of managerial expertise.
- The technical expertise of traders.

- The understanding and adherence to the strategic direction and risk tolerance as defined by senior management, the federal branch's or agency's as well as the head office's.

	Strong	Satisfactory	Weak
Control Systems	•	•	•

- The accuracy, completeness, and integrity of management information systems.
- The adequacy and independence of validation processes for trading models and methods.
- The reasonableness, communication, and monitoring of limit structures.
- The frequency and reliability of revaluations of individual position-taking.
- The potential exposure to trading losses as measured under normal and adverse scenarios.
- The adequacy of internal and external audit.
- The responsiveness of management to internal control deficiencies.
- The responsiveness of control systems to identified deficiencies in policy, process, and personnel.

Foreign Currency Translation Risk

Quantity of Foreign Currency Translation Risk

For federal branches and agencies, foreign currency translation risk mainly occurs at the FBO level. The risk is incurred when the financial statements are converted from the federal branch's or agency's functional currency, i.e., the U.S. dollar, into the reporting currency of the head office. Such translation is normally performed only on reporting dates. At the federal branch or agency level, foreign currency translation risk would occur when nondollar assets or liabilities are held. Foreign currency translation risk would affect the federal branch's or agency's earnings when these assets are converted to the U.S. dollar equivalents. Insured federal branches are permitted to accept deposits denominated in foreign currency. Foreign currency translation risk occurs when the federal branch converts such accounts to the U.S. dollar equivalent for filing regulatory reports with U.S. supervisory agencies. Federal branches should notify customers that such deposits are subject to foreign currency translation risk.

At a minimum, risk assessment factors should be reviewed, monitored, and analyzed during the course of a supervisory cycle (every 12 or 18 months) to ensure quality supervision. Using the core assessment factors, examiners assess whether the risk is low, moderate, or high.

Is there a material amount of earnings at risk from foreign currency translation?

- Yes
- No   If no, skip this section and go to quality of risk management.

	Low	Moderate	High
Structural Factors	•	•	•

- The level of federal branch or agency earnings subject to revaluation from currency translation requirements.
- The potential volatility of federal branch or agency earnings ratios from translating accounts denominated in other currencies to their U.S. dollar equivalent, including an analysis of recent trends and projections.
- The extent of the federal branch's or agency's earnings exposure to foreign currency translation risk considering:

- The volume and stability of portfolios denominated in foreign currencies.
- The level of income items denominated in foreign currencies (e.g., revenues and expenses).
- The mismatching of assets and liabilities denominated in a foreign currency.
- The types of products held in foreign currency accounts (e.g., loans, bonds, derivatives).

	Low	Moderate	High
Strategic Factors	•	•	•

- The effectiveness of hedging activities to control exposure to translation risk by:
  - Matching foreign asset and liability cash flows.
  - Hedging projected income.
  - Using financial contracts (futures, options, etc.)
- The volume and tenor of foreign currency/U.S.-dollar-denominated mismatches.
- The volume and tenor of cross-currency (not involving U.S.-dollar-denominated items) mismatches.
- The vulnerability to the true economic value of the hedging instrument.
- The impact of changes in business strategies as outlined by the head office for the federal branch or agency.

	Low	Moderate	High
External Factor	•	•	•

- The exposure to market volatility or other external factors such as interest rate and inflation rate changes.

Quality of Foreign Currency Translation Risk Management

Examiners should consider the following assessment factors when making judgments about the quality of foreign currency translation risk management. These factors are consistent with the minimum standards that all examiners will consider when completing a risk assessment. They are consistent with the framework for the ongoing supervisory approach used in large banks. At a minimum, they should be reviewed, monitored, and analyzed during the course of a supervisory cycle (every 12 or 18 months) to ensure quality supervision.

Using the core assessment factors, examiners assess whether the risk management is strong, satisfactory, or weak.

	Strong	Satisfactory	Weak
Policies	•	•	•

- The appropriateness of policies to address hedging requirements and standards.
- The adequacy of policies to address the appropriateness and use of monitoring systems.
- The existence of standards that detail the results expected from hedging activities.
- The reasonableness of exposure limits defined within policies.
- The responsibility and accountability for activities that create a foreign currency translation risk operation are clearly defined at the federal branch or agency.
- Federal branch or agency policies should address the foreign currency translation risk limit established by the head office for the federal branch or agency.

	Strong	Satisfactory	Weak
Processes	•	•	•

- The adequacy of internal controls for hedging operations (front and back office) including segregation of duties and dual controls.
- The adequacy of controls over new product development.
- The adequacy of independent measurement and analysis of risk under a variety of scenarios, including stress tests.
- The adequacy of data systems and reports. Examiners should verify that all reports are in order and evaluate the use of such funds and management of the accompanying foreign currency translation risk.
- The processing capabilities of the front and back office systems, considering the current and projected size and scope of foreign-currency-denominated activities.
- The adequacy of federal branch or agency management supervision and head office oversight (e.g., approving, monitoring, and reporting compliance with limits and guidelines, communicating policies and expectations to appropriate personnel).

	Strong	Satisfactory	Weak
Personnel	•	•	•

- The extent of managerial expertise.
- The technical expertise of staff members.
- The understanding and adherence to the strategic direction and risk tolerance as defined by head office management.

	Strong	Satisfactory	Weak
Control Systems	•	•	•

- The accuracy, completeness, and integrity of management information systems.
- The adequacy of internal and external audit.
- The responsiveness of control systems to identified deficiencies in policy, process, and personnel.
- The responsiveness of independent risk and internal control functions to deficiencies.

Transaction Risk

Quantity of Transaction Risk

Examiners should consider the following assessment factors when making judgments about the quantity of transaction risk. These factors are consistent with the minimum standards that all examiners will consider when completing a risk assessment (appendix B). These factors are the framework for the ongoing supervisory approach used in large banks. At a minimum, they should be reviewed, monitored, and analyzed during the course of a supervisory cycle (every 12 or 18 months) to ensure quality supervision. Using the core assessment factors, examiners assess whether the risk is low, moderate, or high.

	Low	Moderate	High
The volume, type, and complexity of transactions, products, and services offered through the federal branch or agency.	•	•	•
The condition, security, capacity, and recoverability of systems.	•	•	•
The complexity of conversions, integrations, and system changes.	•	•	•
The development of new markets, products, services, technology, and delivery systems in order to maintain competitive position and gain strategic advantage.	•	•	•
The volume and severity of operational, administrative, and accounting control exceptions.	•	•	•

Quality of Transaction Risk Management

Examiners should consider the following assessment factors when making judgments about the quality of transaction risk management. These factors are consistent with the minimum standards that all examiners will consider when completing a risk assessment. These factors are consistent with the framework for the ongoing supervisory approach used in large banks. At a minimum, they should be reviewed, monitored, and analyzed during the course of a supervisory cycle (every 12 or 18 months) to ensure quality supervision. Using the core assessment factors, examiners assess whether the risk management is strong, satisfactory, or weak.

	Strong	Satisfactory	Weak
Policies	•	•	•

- The consistency of federal branch or agency policies with the strategic direction of the FBO.
- The structure of the federal branch's or agency's operations and whether responsibility and accountability are assigned at every level.
- The reasonableness of definitions that determine policy exceptions.
- The periodic review and approval of policies by head office management.
- The reasonableness of guidelines that establish risk limits or positions.

	Strong	Satisfactory	Weak
Processes	•	•	•

- The adequacy of processes communicating policies and expectations to appropriate personnel.
- The provision of timely and useful management information systems reports.
- The approval and monitoring of compliance with policies.
- The appropriateness of the approval process.
- Control over the accuracy, completeness, and integrity of data.
- Management's responsiveness to changes in regulation, banking, and technology, such as year-2000 computer refinements.
- The adequacy of business continuity planning.
- The incorporation of project management into daily operations (e.g., systems development, capacity, change control, due diligence, and outsourcing).
- The adequacy of processes defining the systems architecture for transaction processing and for delivering products and services.
- The adequacy of systems to monitor capacity and performance.
- The effectiveness of processes developed to ensure the integrity and security of systems and the independence of operating staff.
- The adequacy of system documentation history.

- The adequacy of processes to ensure the reliability and retention of information, including business continuity planning (e.g., data creation, processing, storage, and delivery).
- The adequacy of internal controls including segregation of duties and dual controls.

	Strong	Satisfactory	Weak
Personnel	•	•	•

- The appropriateness of performance management and compensation programs.
- The level of turnover of critical staff.
- The adequacy of training.
- The extent of managerial expertise.
- The understanding of and adherence to the strategic direction and risk tolerance as defined by management, the federal branch's or agency's as well as the head office's.

	Strong	Satisfactory	Weak
Control Systems	•	•	•

- The effectiveness and independence of risk review, quality assurance, and audit functions.
- The accuracy, completeness, and integrity of management information systems and reports.
- The existence of exception monitoring systems that identify and measure incremental risk by how much (in frequency and amount) the exceptions deviate from policy and established limits.
- The responsiveness to identified internal deficiencies in policy, process, personnel and controls.
- The responsiveness to internal control deficiencies.
- The independent testing of processes to ensure ongoing reliability and integrity.

Compliance Risk

Quantity of Compliance Risk

Examiners should consider the following assessment factors when making judgments about the quantity of compliance risk. These factors are the minimum standards that all examiners will consider when completing a risk assessment (appendix B). These factors are consistent with the framework for the ongoing supervisory approach used in large banks. At a minimum, they should be reviewed, monitored, and analyzed during the course of a supervisory cycle (every 12 or 18 months) to ensure quality supervision. Using the core assessment factors, examiners assess whether the risk is low, moderate, or high.

	Low	Moderate	High
Business Activity	•	•	•

- The nature and extent of business activities, including new products and services.

	Low	Moderate	High
Noncompliance	•	•	•

- The volume and significance of noncompliance and nonconformance with policies and procedures, laws, regulations, prescribed practices, and ethical standards.

	Low	Moderate	High
Litigation	•	•	•

- The amount and significance of litigation and customer complaints.

Quality of Compliance Risk Management

Examiners should consider the following assessment factors when making judgments about the quality of compliance risk management. These factors are the minimum standards that all examiners will consider when completing a risk assessment. These factors are consistent with the framework for the ongoing supervisory approach used in large banks. At a minimum, they should be reviewed, monitored, and analyzed during the course of a supervisory cycle (every 12 or 18 months) to ensure quality supervision. Using the core assessment factors, examiners assess whether the risk management is strong, satisfactory, or weak.

	Strong	Satisfactory	Weak
Policies	•	•	•

- The appropriateness of established risk limits.
- The consistency of policies with the strategic direction of the FBO.
- The structure of the compliance operation and whether responsibility and accountability are assigned at every level.
- The reasonableness of definitions that determine policy exceptions.
- The periodic approval of compliance policies by head office management.

	Strong	Satisfactory	Weak
Processes	•	•	•

- The timely communication of policies and expectations to appropriate personnel.
- The adequacy of controls over new product development.
- The adequacy of data systems and reports.
- The adequacy of management supervision and board oversight.
- The adequacy of internal controls including segregation of duties, dual controls, etc.
- The provision of timely and useful management information systems reports.
- The effectiveness of processes controlling the accuracy, completeness, and integrity of data.
- The adequacy of processes assimilating legislative and regulatory changes into all aspects of the federal branch or agency.
- The commitment to ensuring that appropriate resources are allocated to training and compliance.
- The extent to which violations or noncompliance are identified internally and corrected.
- The adequacy of integrating compliance considerations into all phases of federal branch or agency planning.

	Strong	Satisfactory	Weak
Personnel	•	•	•

- The appropriateness of performance management and compensation programs.
- The degree of turnover of critical staff.
- The adequacy of training.
- The extent of managerial expertise.
- The understanding and adherence to the strategic direction and risk tolerance as defined by federal branch or agency and head office management.

	Strong	Satisfactory	Weak
Control Systems	•	•	•

- The effectiveness and independence of the risk review, quality assurance, and audit functions.
- The accuracy, completeness, and integrity of management information systems and reports.
- The existence of exception monitoring systems that identify and measure incremental risk by how much (in frequency and amount) the exceptions deviate from policy and established limits.
- The responsiveness to identified internal deficiencies in policies, processes, personnel, and controls.
- The responsiveness to internal control deficiencies.

Strategic Risk

Examiners should consider the following assessment factors when making judgments about the aggregate strategic risk. These factors are the minimum standards that all examiners will consider when completing a risk assessment (appendix B). These factors are consistent with the framework for the ongoing supervisory approach used in large banks. At a minimum, they should be reviewed, monitored, and analyzed during the course of a supervisory cycle (every 12 or 18 months) to ensure quality supervision. Using the core assessment factors, examiners assess whether the risk management is low, moderate, or high.

	Low	Moderate	High
Strategic Factors	•	•	•

- The magnitude of change in established corporate mission, goals, culture, values, or risk tolerance established by head office management for the federal branch or agency.
- The financial objectives as they relate to the short- and long-term goals of the federal branch or agency.
- The market situation, including product, customer demographics, and geographic position.
- Diversification by product, geography, and customer demographics.
- Past performance in offering new products and services.
- Merger and acquisition plans and opportunities.
- The FBO's merger and acquisition plans and opportunities.
- Potential or planned entrance into new businesses or product lines by the federal branch or agency and FBO.

	Low	Moderate	High
External Factor	•	•	•

- The impact of economic, industry, and market conditions; legislative and regulatory change; technological advances; and competition.

	Low	Moderate	High
Management, Processes, and Systems	•	•	•

- The expertise of federal branch or agency management and the effectiveness of head office management oversight.

- The priority and compatibility of personnel, technology, and capital resources allocation with strategic initiatives.
- Past performance in offering new products or services.
- The effectiveness of management's methods of communicating, implementing, and modifying strategic plans, and consistency with stated risk tolerance.
- The accuracy, quality, and integrity of management information systems.
- The adequacy and independence of controls to monitor business decisions.
- The responsiveness to deficiencies in internal controls.
- The quality and integrity of reports to head office management necessary to oversee strategic decisions.
- If applicable, the ability to manage fair lending and community reinvestment issues in conjunction with strategic initiatives.

Reputation Risk

Examiners should consider the following assessment factors when making judgments about the aggregate reputation risk. These factors are the minimum standards that all examiners will consider when completing a risk assessment (appendix B). These factors are consistent with the framework for the ongoing supervisory approach used in large banks. At a minimum, they should be reviewed, monitored, and analyzed during the course of a supervisory cycle (every 12 or 18 months) to ensure quality supervision. Using the core assessment factors, examiners assess whether the risk is low, moderate, or high.

	Low	Moderate	High
Strategic Factors	•	•	•

- The volume of assets and number of accounts under management or administration.
- Potential or planned entrance into new businesses or product lines, particularly those that test legal boundaries.
- Head office merger and acquisition plans and opportunities.

	Low	Moderate	High
External Factors	•	•	•

- The market's or public's perception of the corporate mission, culture, and risk tolerance of the FBO.
- The market's or public's perception of the FBO's financial stability.
- The market's or public's perception of the quality of products and services offered by the federal branch or agency.
- The impact of economic, industry, and market conditions; legislative and regulatory change; technological advances; and competition.

	Low	Moderate	High
Management, Processes, and Systems	•	•	•

- Past performance in offering new products or services and in conducting due diligence prior to startup.
- The nature and amount of litigation and customer complaints.

- The expertise of federal branch or agency management and the effectiveness of head office management in maintaining an ethical, self-policing culture.
- The stability of federal branch or agency management and staffing, and the effectiveness of management transition.
- Management's willingness and ability to adjust strategies based on regulatory changes, market disruptions, market or public perception, and legal losses.
- The quality and integrity of management information systems and the development of expanded or newly integrated systems.
- The adequacy and independence of controls used to monitor business decisions.
- The responsiveness to deficiencies in internal controls.
- The ability to minimize exposure from litigation and customer complaints.
- The ability to communicate effectively with the market, public, and media.
- Management's responsiveness to internal and regulatory review findings.

Internal Controls

Examiners should consider the following assessment factors when making judgments about internal controls. These factors are the minimum standards that all examiners will consider during the course of a supervisory cycle (every 12 or 18 months) to ensure quality supervision. Using the core assessment factors, examiners assess whether the risk is strong, satisfactory, or weak.

	Strong	Satisfactory	Weak
Control Environment	•	•	•

- The integrity, ethical values, and competence of personnel.
- The organizational structure of the federal branch or agency.
- Management's philosophy and operating style (e.g., strategic philosophy).
- External influences affecting operations and practices (e.g., independent audits, regulatory environment, and competitive and business markets).
- Methods of assigning authority and responsibility, and organizing and developing people.
- The attention and direction provided by head office management, especially in the areas of audit and risk management.

	Strong	Satisfactory	Weak
Risk Assessment	•	•	•

- External and internal factors that could affect whether strategic objectives are achieved.
- Identification and analysis of risks.
- The system used to manage and monitor the risks.
- Processes that react and respond to changing risk conditions.
- The competency, knowledge, and skills of personnel responsible for risk assessment.

	Strong	Satisfactory	Weak
Control Activities	•	•	•

- Policies and procedures established to ensure control processes are carried out.
- Reviews of operating activities.
- Approvals and authorization for transactions and activities.
- Segregation of duties.
- Vacation requirements or periodic rotation of duties for personnel in sensitive positions.

- Safeguarding access to and use of sensitive assets and records.
- Independent checks or verifications on function performance and reconciliation of balances.
- Accountability.

	Strong	Satisfactory	Weak
Accounting, Information, and Communication	•	•	•

- MIS that identify and capture relevant internal and external information in a timely manner.
- Accounting systems that ensure accountability for related assets and liabilities.
- Information systems that ensure effective communication of positions and activities.
- Contingency planning for information systems.

	Strong	Satisfactory	Weak
Self-assessment and Monitoring	•	•	•

- Periodic evaluation of internal controls whether by self-assessment or independent audit.
- Systems to ensure timely and accurate reporting of deficiencies.
- Processes to ensure timely modification of policies and procedures, as needed.

After considering the above factors, the overall system of internal controls is:

• Strong	• Satisfactory	• Weak

ROCA Rating System

Examiners should consider the following assessment factors when making judgments about ROCA. These factors are the minimum standards that all examiners will consider during the course of a supervisory cycle (every 12 or 18 months) to ensure quality supervision. Examiners should assess whether the individual ROCA components (risk management, operational controls, and compliance), and the quality of the federal branch's or agency's stock of assets as of the examination date, are rated 1, 2, 3, 4, or 5. The individual component ratings are taken into consideration by the examiner in the assessment of an overall or composite rating of the federal branch or agency. (See appendix D for a detailed description of the ROCA rating system).

	1	2	3	4	5
Risk Management	•	•	•	•	•

- The extent to which federal branch or agency management is able to manage the risks inherent in its lending, trading, and other activities; specifically, its ability to identify, measure, and control these risks.
- The soundness of the qualitative and quantitative assumptions implicit in the risk management system.
- Whether risk policies, guidelines, and limits at the federal branch or agency are consistent with its lending, trading, and other activities; management's experience level; and the overall financial strength of the federal branch or agency and/or the FBO.
- Whether the management information systems and other forms of communication are consistent with the level of business activity at the federal branch or agency and sufficient to accurately monitor risk exposure, compliance with established limits, and sufficient to enable the head office to monitor the real performance and risks of the federal branch or agency.
- Management's ability to recognize and accommodate new risks that may arise from the changing environment and to identify and address risks not readily quantified in a risk management system.

	1	2	3	4
5 Operational Controls	•	•	•	•

- The adequacy of controls and the level of adherence to existing procedures and systems (These are separate but related factors).
- The frequency, scope, and adequacy of the federal branch's or agency's internal and external audit function, relative to the size and risk profile of the federal branch or agency, and the independence of the internal audit function from line management.
- The number and severity of internal control and audit exceptions.
- Whether internal control and audit exceptions are effectively tracked and resolved in a timely manner.
- The adequacy and accuracy of management information reports. This assessment should be based primarily on whether reports and analyses are sufficiently detailed to properly inform head office management of the federal branch's or agency's condition on a timely basis, and whether there are sufficient procedures to ensure the accuracy of these reports.
- Whether the system of controls is regularly reviewed to keep pace with changes in the federal branch's or agency's business plan and laws and regulations.

	1	2	3	4
5 Compliance	•	•	•	•

- The level of adherence to applicable state and federal laws and regulations and any supervisory follow-up actions.
- The effectiveness of: (1) written compliance procedures and (2) training of line personnel charged with maintaining compliance with regulatory requirements.
- Management's ability to submit required regulatory reports in a timely and accurate manner.
- Management's ability to identify and correct compliance issues.
- Whether the internal audit function checks for compliance with applicable state and federal laws and regulations.

	1	2	3	4	5
Asset Quality	•	•	•		•
•					

- The level, distribution, and severity of asset and off-balance-sheet exposures classified for credit and/or transfer risk.
- The level and composition of nonaccrual, and reduced rate assets.

Risk Assessment System

Credit Risk

Credit risk is the current and prospective risk to earnings or capital arising from an obligor's failure to meet the terms of any contract with the bank or otherwise perform as agreed. Credit risk is found in all activities where success depends on counterparty, issuer, or borrower performance. It arises any time bank funds are extended, committed, invested, or otherwise exposed through actual or implied contractual agreements, whether reflected on or off the balance sheet.

Summary Conclusions

Conclusions from the core assessment (appendix A) allow examiners to assess the quantity of credit risk, the quality of credit risk management, the aggregate credit risk, and the direction of change. The RAS must be updated at least quarterly or more frequently if prescribed by district office management to reflect the most accurate risk profile of the institution; however, examiners normally will not need to complete in full the core assessment quarterly.

Examiners should consider both the quantity of credit risk and the quality of credit risk management to derive the following conclusions.

Aggregate credit risk is:

• Low	• Moderate	• High

The direction of change is expected to be:

• Decreasing	• Stable	• Increasing

Supporting narrative comment:

> Support all ratings in one narrative comment (i.e., aggregate risk, direction of change expected, quantity of risk, and quality of risk management) in the OCC's electronic information system.

> In the OCC's electronic information system, document any changes in supervisory strategy that are made because of changes in the federal branch's or agency's risk profile.

Quantity of Credit Risk

Examiners should use the following definitions to determine the quantity of credit risk. It is not necessary to exhibit every characteristic to be accorded a specific rating.

The quantity of credit risk is:

> • Low   • Moderate   • High

- Low – Current or prospective exposure to loss of earnings is minimal. Credit exposures reflect conservative structure or marketing initiatives. The volume of substantive exceptions or overrides to sound underwriting standards poses minimal risk. Exposures represent a well- diversified distribution by investment grade (or equivalently strong nonrated borrowers) and borrower leverage. Borrowers operate in stable markets and industries. Risk of loss from concentrations is minimal. Limited sensitivity exists due to deteriorating economic, industry, competitive, regulatory, and technological factors. Compensation is adequate to justify the risk being assumed. Portfolio growth presents no concerns. Credit-related losses do not meaningfully impact current reserves and result in modest provisions relative to earnings.

- Moderate – Current or prospective exposure to loss of earnings does not materially impact financial condition. Credit exposures reflect acceptable underwriting or marketing initiatives. Substantive exceptions or overrides to sound underwriting standards may exist, but do not pose advanced risk. Exposures may include non-investment grade (or equivalently strong nonrated borrowers) or leveraged borrowers, but borrowers typically operate in less volatile markets and industries.

Exposure does not reflect significant concentrations. Vulnerability may exist due to deteriorating economic, industry, competitive, regulatory, and technological factors. Compensation is adequate to justify the risk being assumed. While advanced portfolio growth may exist within specific products or sectors, it is in accordance with a reasonable plan. Credit-related losses do not seriously deplete current reserves or necessitate large provisions relative to earnings.

• High — Current or prospective exposure to loss of earnings is material. Credit exposures reflect aggressive underwriting or marketing initiatives. A large volume of substantive exceptions or overrides to sound underwriting standards exist. Exposures are skewed toward non-investment grade (or equivalently strong nonrated borrowers) or highly leveraged borrowers, or borrowers operating in volatile markets and industries. Exposure reflects significant concentrations. Significant vulnerability exists due to deteriorating economic, industry, competitive, regulatory, and technological factors. Compensation is inadequate to justify the risk being assumed. Portfolio growth, including products or sectors within the portfolio, is aggressive. Credit-related losses may seriously deplete current reserves or necessitate large provisions relative to earnings.

Quality of Credit Risk Management

Examiners should use the following definitions to determine the quality of credit risk management. It is not necessary to meet every qualifier to be accorded a specific rating.

The quality of credit risk management is:

• Strong	• Satisfactory	• Weak

• Strong – The credit policy function comprehensively defines risk tolerance, responsibilities, and accountability. All aspects of credit policies are effectively communicated. The credit culture, including compensation, strikes an appropriate balance between marketing and credit considerations. The credit granting process is extensively defined, well understood and adhered to consistently. Credit analysis is thorough and timely. Risk measurement and monitoring systems are comprehensive and allow management to proactively implement appropriate actions in response to changes in asset quality and market conditions. Credit risk information systems are sophisticated, effectively integrated into the risk management process, and regularly updated. Internal grading and reporting accurately stratifies credit quality. Credit administration is effective. Management identifies and actively manages portfolio risk, including the risk relating to credit structure and concentrations. The ALLL methodology is well defined, objective and clearly supports adequacy of current reserve levels. Personnel possess extensive technical and managerial expertise. Internal controls are comprehensive and effective. The stature, quality, and independence of internal loan review and audit support highly effective control systems.

- Satisfactory – The credit policy function satisfactorily defines risk tolerance, responsibilities, and accountability. Key aspects of credit policies are effectively communicated. The credit culture, including compensation, appropriately balances marketing and credit considerations. The credit granting process is well defined and understood. Credit analysis is adequate. Risk measurement and monitoring systems permit management to capably respond to changes in asset quality or market conditions. Credit risk information systems are satisfactory. Internal grading and reporting accurately stratifies portfolio quality. Credit administration is adequate. Management can identify and monitor portfolio risk, including the risk relating to credit structure. Management's attention to credit risk diversification is adequate. The ALLL methodology is satisfactory and results in sufficient coverage of inherent credit losses. Personnel possess requisite technical and managerial expertise. Key internal controls are in place and effective. The stature, quality, and independence of internal loan review and audit is appropriate.

- Weak – The credit policy function may not effectively define risk tolerance, responsibilities, and accountability. Credit policies are not effectively communicated. The credit culture, including compensation, overemphasizes marketing relative to credit considerations. The credit granting process is not well defined or not well understood. Credit analysis is insufficient relative to the risk. Risk measurement and monitoring systems may not permit management to implement timely and appropriate actions in response to changes in asset quality or market conditions. Credit risk information systems may be deficient. Internal grading and reporting of credit exposure does not accurately stratify the portfolio's quality. Credit administration is ineffective. Management is unable to identify and monitor portfolio risk, including the risk relating to credit structure. Management's attention to credit risk diversification is inadequate. The ALLL methodology is flawed and may result in insufficient coverage of inherent credit losses. Personnel lack requisite technical and managerial expertise. Key internal controls may be absent or ineffective. The stature, quality, or independence of internal loan review and/or audit is lacking.

Interest Rate Risk

Interest rate risk (IRR) is the current and prospective risk to earnings or capital arising from movements in interest rates. Interest rate risk arises from differences between the timing of rate changes and the timing of cash flows (repricing risk), from changing rate relationships among different yield curves affecting bank activities (basis risk), from changing rate relationships across the spectrum of maturities (yield curve risk), and from interest-related options embedded in bank products (options risk).

Summary Conclusions

Conclusions from the core assessment (appendix A) allow examiners to assess the quantity of interest rate risk, the quality of interest rate risk management, the aggregate interest rate risk, and the direction of change. The RAS must be updated at least quarterly or more frequently if prescribed by district office management to reflect the most accurate risk profile of the institution; however, examiners normally will not need to complete the core assessment in full quarterly.

Examiners should consider both the quantity of interest rate risk and the quality of interest rate risk management to derive the following conclusions.

Aggregate interest rate risk is:

• Low	• Moderate	• High

The direction of change is expected to be:

• Decreasing	• Stable	• Increasing

Supporting Narrative Comment:

Support all ratings in one narrative comment (i.e., aggregate risk, direction of change expected, quantity of risk, and quality of risk management) in the OCC's electronic information system.

> In the OCC's electronic information system, document any changes in supervisory strategy that are made because of changes in the federal branch's or agency's risk profile.

Quantity of Interest Rate Risk

Examiners should use the following definitions to determine the quantity of interest rate risk managed at the federal branch or agency level. It is not necessary to meet every qualifier to be accorded a specific rating.

The quantity of interest rate risk is:

• Low	• Moderate	• High

- Low – Exposure reflects minimal repricing, basis, yield curve, and options risk. Positions used to manage interest rate risk exposure are well correlated to underlying risks. No significant mismatches on longer term positions exist. The current or future volatility of earnings is relatively insensitive to changes in interest rates or the exercise of options. Interest rate movements will have minimal adverse impact on the federal branch's or agency's earnings.

- Moderate – Exposure reflects manageable repricing, basis, yield curve, and options risk. Positions used to manage interest rate risk exposure are somewhat correlated. Mismatches on longer term positions are managed. The volatility in earnings is not significantly effected by changes in interest rates or the exercise of options. Interest rate movements will not have a significant adverse impact on the federal branch's or agency's earnings.

- High — Exposure reflects significant repricing, basis, yield curve, or options risk. Positions used to manage interest rate risk exposure are poorly correlated. Significant mismatches on longer term positions exist. Current or future volatility in earnings due to changes in interest rates or the exercise of options are substantial. Interest rate movements could have a significant adverse impact on the federal branch's or agency's earnings.

Quality of Interest Rate Risk Management

Examiners should use the following definitions to determine the quality of interest rate risk management. It is not necessary to meet every qualifier to be accorded a specific rating.

The quality of interest rate risk management is:

• Strong	• Satisfactory	• Weak

- Strong – Management fully understands all aspects of interest rate risk management from the earnings and economic perspectives, as appropriate. Discretionary risk positions are effectively measured and controlled. Management anticipates and quickly responds to changes in market conditions. Interest rate risk is well understood at all appropriate levels of the federal branch or agency and head office. The interest rate risk management process is effective and proactive. Measurement tools and methods are appropriate given the size and complexity of the federal branch's or agency's on- and off-balance-sheet exposures and enhance decision making by providing meaningful and timely information under a variety of defined and reasonable rate scenarios. Few, if any, weaknesses or deficiencies exist. Management information at various levels of the federal branch or agency is timely, accurate, complete, and reliable. Limit structures provide clear parameters for risk to earnings under normal and adverse scenarios. Staff responsible for measuring exposures and monitoring risk limits are independent from staff executing risk-taking decisions.

- Satisfactory – Management reasonably understands the key aspects of interest rate risk management from the earnings and economic perspectives, as appropriate. Discretionary risk positions are properly measured and controlled. Management adequately responds to changes in market conditions. Knowledge of interest rate risk exists at appropriate levels throughout the federal branch or agency and head office. The interest rate risk management process is adequate. Measurement tools and methods may have minor weaknesses, but are appropriate given the size and complexity of the federal branch's or agency's on- and off-balance-sheet exposures. Management information at various levels in the federal branch or agency is satisfactory, given the nature of the federal branch's or agency's activities. Limit structures are reasonable and sufficient to control the risk to earnings under normal and adverse interest rate scenarios. Staff responsible for measuring exposures and monitoring risk are independent from staff executing risk-taking decisions.

- Weak – Management may not satisfactorily understand interest rate risk management from the earnings or economic perspective. Discretionary risk positions are not adequately measured or controlled. Management does not take timely or appropriate actions in response to changes in market conditions. Knowledge of interest rate risk may be lacking at appropriate management levels throughout the federal branch or agency and head office. The interest rate risk management process is deficient, given the relative size and complexity of the federal branch's or agency's on- and off-balance-sheet exposures. Measurement tools and methods are inadequate or inappropriate given the size and complexity of the federal branch's or agency's on- and off-balance-sheet exposures. Management information at various levels in the federal branch or agency exhibits significant weaknesses and may not consolidate total exposures. Limit structures are not reasonable, or do not reflect an understanding of the risks to earnings under normal and adverse scenarios. Staff responsible for measuring exposures and monitoring risk are not independent from staff executing risk-taking decisions.

Liquidity Risk

Liquidity risk is the current and prospective risk to earnings or capital arising from a bank's inability to meet its obligations when they come due without incurring unacceptable losses. Liquidity risk includes the inability to manage unplanned decreases or changes in funding sources. Liquidity risk also arises from the failure to recognize or address changes in market conditions that affect the ability to liquidate assets quickly and with minimal loss in value.

Summary Conclusions

Conclusions from the core assessment (appendix A) allow examiners to assess the quantity of liquidity risk, the quality of liquidity risk management, the aggregate liquidity risk, and the direction of change. The RAS must be updated at least quarterly or more frequently if prescribed by district office management to reflect the most accurate risk profile of the institution; however, examiners normally will not need to complete the core assessment in full quarterly.

Examiners should consider both the quantity of liquidity risk and the quality of liquidity risk management to derive the following conclusions.

Aggregate liquidity risk is:

• Low	• Moderate	• High

The direction of change is expected to be:

• Decreasing	• Stable	• Increasing

Supporting narrative comment:

> Support all ratings in one narrative comment (i.e., aggregate risk, direction of change expected, quantity of risk, and quality of risk management) in the OCC's electronic information system.

> In the OCC's electronic information system, document any changes in supervisory strategy that are made because of changes in the federal branch's or agency's risk profile.

Quantity of Liquidity Risk

Examiners should use the following definitions to determine the quantity of liquidity risk. It is not necessary to meet every qualifier to be accorded a specific rating.

The quantity of liquidity risk is:

> • Low • Moderate • High

- Low – The federal branch or agency is not vulnerable to funding difficulties should a material adverse change in market perception occur. Earnings exposure from the liquidity risk profile is negligible. Sources of deposits and borrowings are widely diversified, with no material concentrations. Ample funding sources and structural cash flow symmetry exist in all tenors. Stable deposits and a strong market acceptance of the FBO's name offer the federal branch or agency a competitive liability cost advantage. Reasonable alternatives to credit-sensitive funding, if relied upon, have been identified by management and can easily be implemented with no disruption in strategic lines of business.

- Moderate – The federal branch or agency is not excessively vulnerable to funding difficulties should a material adverse change in market perception occur. Earnings exposure from the liquidity risk profile is manageable. Sources of funding are reasonably diverse but minor concentrations may exist, and funds providers may be moderately credit sensitive. Some groups of providers may share common investment objectives or be subject to similar economic influences. Sufficient funding sources, and structural balance sheet and cash flow symmetry exist to provide stable, cost-effective liquidity in most environments, without significant disruption in strategic lines of business.

- High – The federal branch's or agency's liquidity profile makes it vulnerable to funding difficulties should a material adverse change occur. Significant concentrations of funding may exist, or there may be a significant volume of providers that are highly credit-sensitive. Large funds providers may share common investment objectives or be subject to similar economic influences. The federal branch or agency may currently, or potentially, experience market resistance which could impact its ability to access needed funds at a reasonable cost. As a result, the federal branch or agency may become dependent on the head office's ability to make funds available. There may be an increasing demand for liquidity with declining medium- and long-term alternatives. Funding sources and balance sheet structures may currently result in, or suggest, potential difficulty in sustaining long-term liquidity on a cost-effective basis. A downgrade in the home country's risk rating and the FBO's debt rating has severely affected the federal branch's or agency's funding sources. Potential exposure to loss of earnings due to high liability costs or unplanned asset reduction may be substantial. Liquidity needs may trigger the necessity for funding alternatives under a contingency funding plan, including the sale of or disruption in a strategic line of business.

Quality of Liquidity Risk Management

Examiners should use the following definitions to determine the quality of liquidity risk management at the federal branch or agency. It is not necessary to meet every qualifier to be accorded a specific rating.

The quality of liquidity risk management is:

• Strong	• Satisfactory	• Weak

- Strong – Management proactively incorporates all key aspects of liquidity risk into its overall risk management process, and anticipates and responds promptly to changing market conditions. Management has clearly articulated policies that provide clear insight and guidance on appropriate risk-taking and management. Management information is timely, complete, focused, and reliable. Liquidity planning is fully integrated with strategic planning, budgeting, and financial management processes. Management gives appropriate attention to managing balance sheet symmetry, cash flows, cost effectiveness, and evaluating liquidity alternatives. A comprehensive contingency funding plan exists which is fully integrated into overall risk management processes, and which will enable federal branch or agency management to respond to potential crisis situations in a timely manner.

- Satisfactory – Management reasonably incorporates most of the key aspects of liquidity risk. Management adequately responds to changes in market conditions. Liquidity risk management policies and practices are adequate. Liquidity planning is integrated with the strategic planning, budgeting, and financial management processes. Management information is generally timely, complete, and reliable. Management realistically assesses the funding markets and pays sufficient attention to diversification. Management attention to balance sheet symmetry, cash flow, and cost effectiveness is generally appropriate. Management has a satisfactory contingency funding plan to manage liquidity risk and is generally prepared to manage potential crisis situations.

- Weak – Management does not satisfactorily address key aspects of liquidity risk. Management is not anticipating or implementing timely or appropriate actions in response to changes in market conditions. Liquidity planning is not sufficiently integrated in the strategic planning, budgeting, and financial management processes. Management information systems may be deficient. Management has not realistically assessed the federal branch's or agency's access to the funding markets, has paid insufficient attention to diversification, or has limited awareness of large funds providers and their sensitivity. Management attention to balance sheet and cash flow symmetry is inadequate. The contingency planning process is deficient, inhibiting management's ability to minimize liquidity problems in a deteriorating scenario or to manage potential crisis situations. Management's evaluation of liquidity alternatives does not adequately consider cost effectiveness or the availability of these alternatives in a variety of market environments. The federal branch's or agency's internal risk management systems are acceptable, but the external risks to the federal branch or agency have significantly increased beyond management's control.

Price Risk

Price risk is the risk to earnings or capital arising from changes in the value of traded portfolios of financial instruments. This risk arises from market-making, dealing, and position-taking in interest rate, foreign exchange, equity, and commodities markets.

Summary Conclusions

Conclusions from the core assessment (appendix A) allow examiners to assess the quantity of price risk, the quality of price risk management, the aggregate price risk, and the direction of change. The RAS must be updated at least quarterly or more frequently if prescribed by district office management to reflect the most accurate risk profile of the institution; however, examiners normally will not need to complete the core assessment in full quarterly.

Examiners should consider both the quantity of price risk and the quality of price risk management to derive the following conclusions.

Aggregate price risk is:

• Low	• Moderate	• High

The direction of change is expected to be:

• Decreasing	• Stable	• Increasing

Supporting narrative comment:

> Support all ratings in one narrative comment (i.e., aggregate risk, direction of change expected, quantity of risk, and quality of risk management) in the OCC's electronic information system.

> In the OCC's electronic information system, document any changes in supervisory strategy that are made because of changes in the federal branch's or agency's risk profile.

Quantity of Price Risk

Examiners should use the following definitions to determine the quantity of price risk. It is not necessary to meet every qualifier to be accorded a specific rating.

The quantity of price risk is:

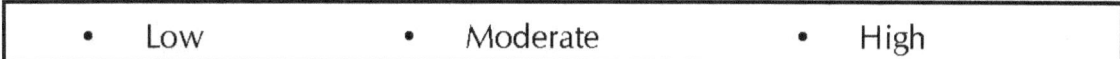

| • Low | • Moderate | • High |

- Low – Exposure reflects limited open or illiquid price risk positions. As a result, earnings are not vulnerable to significant loss. Exposure, whether arising from speculative or customer-driven transactions, involves liquid and readily manageable products, markets, and levels of activity.

- Moderate – Exposure, whether arising from speculative or customer-driven transactions, reflects moderate open or illiquid price risk positions, limiting the potential for significant loss to earnings. The federal branch or agency has access to a variety of risk management instruments and markets at reasonable costs, given the size, tenor, and complexity of open positions.

- High – Exposure reflects significant open or illiquid price risk positions, exposing the federal branch or agency to a significant loss of earnings. Exposure may arise from transactions or positions that are taken as a result of management or trader views of the market, in conjunction with customer transactions, or from market-making activities. Exposures may be difficult or costly to close out or hedge due to size, complexity, or generally illiquid markets, tenors, or products.

Quality of Price Risk Management

Examiners should use the following definitions to determine the quality of price risk management. It is not necessary to meet every qualifier to be accorded a specific rating.

The quality of price risk management is:

• Strong	• Satisfactory	• Weak

- Strong – Several members of federal branch or agency management fully understand price risk. Management actively monitors and understands products, market trends, and changes in market conditions. Management information at various levels within the branch or agency and head office provides a clear assessment of price risk, aggregate risk levels, and addresses limit compliance and exceptions. Models and methodologies are independently validated, tested, and documented. There is a sound independent valuation process for all significant positions. Management fully researches and documents the risk of new product initiatives prior to implementation. Limit structures are reasonable, clear, and effectively communicated. The limits also reflect a clear understanding of the risk to earnings under normal and adverse scenarios. Staff responsible for measuring and monitoring price risk is well qualified and independent from risk-taking activities.

- Satisfactory – Management understands the key aspects of price risk. Management adequately responds to changes in market conditions. Price risk management processes address major exposures. Risk measurement tools and methods may have minor deficiencies or weaknesses, but are sufficient, given the size and complexity of activities. Management information reasonably portrays risk positions and addresses limit compliance and exceptions. Models and methodologies are validated and acceptable. Positions are independently valued. Management considers the risk of new product initiatives prior to implementation. Limit structures are reasonable, clear, and effectively communicated. Limits also reflect an understanding of the risk to earnings under normal and adverse scenarios. Staff responsible for measuring and monitoring price risk are qualified and independent from risk-taking activities.

- Weak – Management does not satisfactorily address key aspects of price risk. Management is not implementing timely or appropriate actions in response to changes in market conditions. Knowledge of price risk may be lacking at appropriate management levels throughout the branch or agency and head office. The price risk management process is deficient in one or more of the following ways. Risk measurement tools and methods are inadequate given the size and complexity of activities.

Management information at various levels within the federal branch or agency and head office does not accurately characterize risk positions, or address limit compliance and exceptions. Position valuations are performed infrequently, exclude major products, or may not be sufficiently independent. Management does not adequately consider the risk of new product initiatives prior to implementation. Limit structures may not be reasonable, clear, or effectively communicated. Limits also may not reflect a complete understanding of the risk to earnings. Staff responsible for measuring and monitoring price risk are not independent of risk-taking activities.

Foreign Currency Translation Risk

Foreign currency translation risk is the current and prospective risk to capital or earnings arising from the conversion of a bank's financial statements from one currency to another. It refers to the variability in accounting values for a bank's equity accounts that results from variations in exchange rates which are used in translating carrying values and income streams in foreign currencies to U.S. dollars. Market-making and position-taking in foreign currencies should be captured under price risk. As previously stated, in the case of a federal branch or agency, foreign currency translation risk is an earnings impact.

Summary Conclusions

Conclusions from the core assessment (appendix A) should allow examiners to assess the quantity of foreign currency translation risk, the quality of foreign currency translation risk management, the aggregate foreign currency translation risk, and the direction of change. The RAS must be updated at least quarterly or more frequently if prescribed by district office management to reflect the most accurate risk profile of the institution; however, examiners normally will not need to complete the core assessment in full quarterly.

Examiners should consider both the quantity of foreign currency translation risk and the quality of foreign currency translation risk management to derive the following conclusions.

Aggregate foreign currency translation risk is: Not Applicable •

• Low	• Moderate	• High

The direction of change is expected to be:

• Decreasing	• Stable	• Increasing

Supporting narrative comment:

> Support all ratings in one narrative comment (i.e., aggregate risk, direction of change expected, quantity of risk, and quality of risk management) in the OCC's electronic information system.

> In the OCC's electronic information system, document any changes in supervisory strategy that are made because of changes in the federal branch's or agency's risk profile.

Quantity of Foreign Currency Translation Risk

Examiners should use the following definitions to obtain an understanding of the quantity of the federal branch's or agency's foreign currency translation risk. It is not necessary to meet every qualifier to be accorded a specific rating.

The quantity of foreign currency translation risk is:

> - Low   •   Moderate   •   High

- Low – The federal branch or agency is exposed to foreign currencies, but translation adjustments will have an immaterial impact on its earnings. The FBO's foreign translation risk will have an immaterial impact on its condition and, consequently, its ability to serve as a source of support to the federal branch or agency.

- Moderate –The federal branch or agency is exposed to foreign currencies, but translation adjustments are not expected to have an adverse impact on its earnings. The FBO's foreign translation risk is not expected to have an adverse impact on its condition, and, consequently, its ability to serve as a source of support to the federal branch or agency.

- High – Exposure to foreign currencies could produce accounting translation adjustments which will have a material adverse impact on the federal branch's or agency's earnings. The FBO's foreign translation risk is expected to have a material adverse impact on its condition, and, consequently, its ability to serve as a source of support to the federal branch or agency.

Quality of Foreign Currency Translation Risk Management

Examiners should use the following definitions to determine the quality of foreign currency translation risk management. It is not necessary to meet every qualifier to be accorded a specific rating.

The quality of foreign currency translation risk management is:

- Strong – Management fully understands all aspects of foreign currency translation risk. Management anticipates and responds well to changes in market conditions. Exposures are effectively measured, actively managed and monitored independently.

- Satisfactory – Management understands the key aspects of foreign currency translation risk. Management recognizes and responds to changes in market conditions. Exposures are adequately measured and controlled.

- Weak – Management does not satisfactorily address key aspects of foreign currency translation risk. Management is not anticipating or implementing timely or appropriate actions in response to changes in market conditions. Exposures are not measured, managed effectively, or monitored independently.

Transaction Risk

Transaction risk is the current and prospective risk to earnings and capital arising from fraud, error, and the inability to deliver products or services, maintain a competitive position, and manage information. Risk is inherent in efforts to gain strategic advantage, and in the failure to keep pace with changes in the financial services marketplace. Transaction risk is evident in each product and service offered. Transaction risk encompasses: product development and delivery, transaction processing, systems development, computing systems, complexity of products and services, and the internal control environment.

Summary Conclusions

Conclusions from the core assessment (appendix A) allow examiners to assess the quantity of transaction risk, the quality of transaction risk management, the aggregate transaction risk, and the direction of change. The RAS must be updated at least quarterly or more frequently if prescribed by district office management to reflect the most accurate risk profile of the institution; however, examiners normally will not need to complete the core assessment in full quarterly.

Examiners should consider both the quantity of transaction risk and the quality of transaction risk management to derive the following conclusions.

Aggregate transaction risk is:

• Low	• Moderate	• High

The direction of change is expected to be:

• Decreasing	• Stable	• Increasing

Supporting narrative comment:

> Support all ratings in one narrative comment (i.e., aggregate risk, direction of change expected, quantity of risk, and quality of risk management) in the OCC's electronic information system.

> In the OCC's electronic information system, document any changes in supervisory strategy that are made because of changes in the federal branch's or agency's risk profile.

Quantity of Transaction Risk

Examiners should use the following definitions to determine the quantity of transaction risk. It is not necessary to meet every qualifier to be accorded a specific rating.

The quantity of transaction risk is:

> • Low   • Moderate   • High

- Low — The level of transaction processing, complexity of operations, and the state of systems development expose the federal branch or agency to negligible reputation risk and loss of earnings. The volume and complexity of products and services expose the federal branch or agency to minimal risk from fraud or error, processing disruptions, control failures, or system development weaknesses. Risk from planned strategic initiatives is minimal.

- Moderate — The level of transaction processing, complexity of operations, and the state of systems development expose the federal branch or agency to increased reputation risk or loss of earnings. The volume and complexity of products and services raise potential risks from fraud or error, processing disruptions, control failures, or system development weaknesses. Risk from planned strategic initiatives exists, but is manageable.

- High — The level of transaction processing, complexity of operations, and state of systems development expose the federal branch or agency to significant damage to reputation or loss of earnings. The volume and complexity of products and services significantly raise potential risks from fraud or error, processing disruptions, control failures, or systems development weaknesses. Risk is heightened by planned strategic initiatives (e.g., conversions, merger integration, emerging products, and technology).

Quality of Transaction Risk Management

Examiners should use the following definitions to determine the quality of transaction risk management. It is not necessary to meet every qualifier to be accorded a specific rating.

The quality of transaction risk management is:

• Strong	• Satisfactory	• Weak

- Strong — Management anticipates and responds to key aspects of risk associated with operational changes, systems development, and emerging technologies. The federal branch's or agency's systems and processes effectively address exposure to transaction risks. Management has implemented sound information systems, internal controls, and audit coverage, although minor deficiencies may exist. Risks from new products, services, and planned strategic initiatives are well controlled.

- Satisfactory — Management satisfactorily addresses key aspects of risk. Management adequately responds to risks associated with operational changes, systems development, and emerging technology. Systems and processes adequately address significant transaction risks. Operating processes, information systems, internal controls, and audit coverage are satisfactory although deficiencies exist. Management has implemented controls that mitigate risks from new products, services, or planned strategic initiatives.

- Weak — Management may not satisfactorily address key aspects of transaction risk. Management does not anticipate or implement appropriate actions to respond to the increasing complexity of operations, systems development needs, or emerging technology. Systems and processes to control transaction risk are ineffective and may need substantial enhancement. Significant weaknesses exist in operations, information systems, internal controls, or audit coverage. Inadequate planning or due diligence expose the federal branch or agency to significant risk from activities such as the introduction of new products and services or planned strategic initiatives.

Compliance Risk

Compliance risk is the current and prospective risk to earnings or capital arising from violations of, or nonconformance with, laws, rules, regulations, prescribed practices, internal policies and procedures, or ethical standards. Compliance risk also arises in situations where the laws or rules governing certain bank products or activities of the bank's clients may be ambiguous or untested. This risk exposes the institution to fines, civil money penalties, payment of damages, and the voiding of contracts. Compliance risk can lead to diminished reputation, reduced franchise value, limited business opportunities, reduced expansion potential, and lack of contract enforceability.

Summary Conclusions

Conclusions from the core assessment (appendix A) allow examiners to assess the quantity of compliance risk, the quality of compliance risk management, the aggregate compliance risk, and the direction of change. The RAS must be updated at least quarterly or more frequently if prescribed by district office management to reflect the most accurate risk profile of the institution; however, examiners normally will not need to complete the core assessment in full quarterly.

Examiners should consider both the quantity of compliance risk and the quality of compliance risk management to derive the following conclusions.

Aggregate compliance risk is:

• Low	• Moderate	• High

The direction of change is expected to be:

• Decreasing	• Stable	• Increasing

Supporting narrative comment:

> Support all ratings in one narrative comment (i.e., aggregate risk, direction of change expected, quantity of risk, and quality of risk management) in the OCC's electronic information system.

> In the OCC's electronic information system, document any changes in supervisory strategy that are made because of changes in the federal branch's or agency's risk profile.

Quantity of Compliance Risk

Examiners should use the following definitions to determine the quantity of compliance risk. It is not necessary to meet every qualifier to be accorded a specific rating.

The quantity of compliance risk is:

• Low	• Moderate	• High

- Low — The nature and extent of business activities limit the federal branch's or agency's potential exposure to violations or noncompliance. The federal branch or agency has few violations. Violations will not impact reputation, value, earnings, or business opportunity. The branch's or agency's history of complaints or litigation is good.

- Moderate — The nature and extent of business activities may increase the potential for violations or noncompliance. The federal branch or agency may have violations outstanding which are correctable in the normal course of business without impacting reputation, value, earnings, or business opportunity. The federal branch's or agency's history of complaints or litigation is not a concern.

- High — The nature and extent of business activities significantly increase the potential for serious or frequent violations or noncompliance. The federal branch or agency may have substantive violations outstanding which could impact reputation, value, earnings, or business opportunity. The federal branch or agency may have a history of serious complaints or litigation.

Quality of Compliance Risk Management

Examiners should use the following definitions to determine the quality of compliance risk management. It is not necessary to meet every qualifier to be accorded a specific rating.

The quality of compliance risk management is:

• Strong	• Satisfactory	• Weak

• Strong — Management anticipates and addresses key aspects of compliance risk. Management takes timely and effective actions in response to compliance issues or regulatory changes. Compliance management systems are good. Management provides substantial resources and has established and timely enforced accountability for compliance performance. Compliance considerations are an integral part of product or system developments.

• Satisfactory — Management addresses key aspects of compliance risk. Management takes appropriate actions in response to compliance issues or regulatory changes. Compliance management systems are adequate. Management provides appropriate resources and has established or enforced accountability for compliance performance. Compliance considerations are incorporated into product or system developments.

• Weak — Management does not satisfactorily address key aspects of compliance risk. Management is not anticipating or implementing timely or appropriate actions in response to compliance issues or regulatory changes. Compliance management systems are deficient. Management has not provided adequate resources or training, and/or has not established or enforced accountability for compliance performance. Errors are often not detected internally, or corrective actions are often ineffective. Compliance considerations are not incorporated into product or system developments.

Strategic Risk

Strategic risk is the current and prospective impact on earnings or capital arising from adverse business decisions, improper implementation of decisions, or lack of responsiveness to industry changes. This risk is a function of the compatibility of an organization's strategic goals, the business strategies developed to achieve those goals, the resources deployed against these goals, and the quality of implementation. The resources needed to carry out business strategies are both tangible and intangible. They include communication channels, operating systems, delivery networks, and managerial capacities and capabilities. The organization's internal characteristics must be evaluated against the impact of economic, technological, competitive, regulatory, and other environmental changes.

Summary Conclusions

Conclusions from the core assessment (appendix A) allow examiners to assess the composite strategic risk and the direction of change. The RAS must be updated at least quarterly or more frequently if prescribed by district office management to reflect the most accurate risk profile of the institution; however, examiners normally will not need to complete the core assessment in full quarterly.

Composite strategic risk is:

• Low	• Moderate	• High

The direction of change is expected to be:

• Decreasing	• Stable	• Increasing

Supporting narrative comment:

Support ratings in one narrative comment in the OCC's electronic information system.

In the OCC's electronic information system, document any changes in supervisory strategy that are made because of changes in the federal branch's or agency's risk profile.

Examiners should use the following definitions to determine the composite strategic risk. It is not necessary to meet every qualifier to be accorded a specific rating.

- Low – The impact of strategic decisions or external pressures is expected to nominally affect franchise value. Exposure reflects strategic goals that are sound, and are very compatible with business direction and a changing environment. Initiatives are well conceived and supported by systems and management resources for the foreseeable future. Strategic direction and organizational efficiency are enhanced by the depth of management talent. Management has been successful in accomplishing past goals. Initiatives are supported by sound due diligence and effective risk management systems. Strategic decisions can be reversed without significant cost or difficulty. Strategic goals and the corporate culture are effectively communicated and consistently applied throughout the federal branch or agency. Management information systems effectively support strategic direction and initiatives.

- Moderate – The impact of strategic decisions or external pressures is not expected to significantly affect franchise value. Exposure reflects strategic goals that may be aggressive but compatible with the federal branch's or agency's direction and responsive to changes in the environment. Initiatives are supported systems and management resources for the foreseeable future. Management has demonstrated the ability to implement goals and objectives. Management has a reasonable record in decision making and controls. Strategic decisions can be reversed without significant cost or difficulty. The quality of due diligence and risk management is consistent with the strategic issues confronting the federal branch or agency. Strategic goals and the corporate culture are appropriately communicated and consistently applied throughout the organization. Management information systems reasonably support the federal branch's or agency's strategic direction.

- High – The impact of strategic decisions or external pressures is expected to adversely affect franchise value. Strategic initiatives may be overly aggressive or incompatible with business direction. Strategic goals may be nonexistent, poorly defined, or fail to consider changes in the business environment. These weaknesses significantly increase the need for a proper balance between head office management's tolerance for risk and willingness to supply supporting resources. Emphasis on substantive growth or expansion may result in earnings volatility. Management or available resources may be insufficient to accomplish planned initiatives or to make necessary competitive changes. Less than effective risk management systems and lack of adequate due diligence has resulted in deficiencies in management decision making abilities and may undermine effective evaluation of resources and commitment to new products and services, or acquisitions. Strategic decisions may be difficult or costly to reverse. Strategic goals and the corporate culture may not be clearly communicated and consistently applied throughout the organization. Management information systems may be insufficient to support the federal branch's or agency's strategic direction or address a changing environment.

Reputation Risk

Reputation risk is the current and prospective impact on earnings and capital arising from negative public opinion. This affects the institution's ability to establish new relationships or services or continue servicing existing relationships. This risk may expose the institution to litigation, financial loss, or a decline in its customer base. Reputation risk exposure is present throughout the organization and includes the responsibility to exercise an abundance of caution in dealing with customers and the community.

Summary Conclusions

Conclusions from the core assessment (appendix A) allow examiners to assess the composite reputation risk and the direction of change. The RAS should be updated at least quarterly or more frequently if prescribed by district office management to reflect the most accurate risk profile of the institution; however, examiners normally will not need to complete the core assessment in full quarterly.

Composite reputation risk is:

• Low	• Moderate	• High

The direction of change is expected to be:

• Decreasing	• Stable	• Increasing

Supporting narrative comment:

Support ratings in one narrative comment in the OCC's electronic information system.

In the OCC's electronic information system, document any changes in supervisory strategy that are made because of changes in the federal branch's or agency's risk profile.

Examiners should use the following definitions to determine the composite reputation risk. It is not necessary to meet every qualifier to be accorded a specific rating.

- Low – Vulnerability to changes in market and public perception is nominal due to favorable market and public perception of the institution. The level of litigation, losses, and customer complaints is minimal. The potential exposure to franchise value is nominal relative to the number of accounts, the volume of assets under management, and the number of affected transactions. Management anticipates and responds well to changes of a market or regulatory nature that impact its reputation in the marketplace. Management fosters a sound culture and administrative procedures and processes that are well supported throughout the federal branch or agency and have proven very successful over time. Management is well versed in complex risks and has avoided conflicts of interest and other legal or control breaches. Management information systems, internal controls, and audit are very effective.

- Moderate – Vulnerability to changes in market and public perception is not material given the level of litigation, losses, and customer complaints. The potential exposure is manageable and commensurate with the volume of business conducted. Management adequately responds to changes of a market or regulatory nature that impact the institution's reputation in the marketplace. Management has a good record of self-policing and correcting problems. Any deficiencies in management information systems are minor. Administration procedures and processes are satisfactory. The federal branch or agency has avoided conflicts of interest and other legal or control breaches. Risk management processes, internal controls, and audit are generally effective.

- High – Vulnerability to changes in market and public perception is material in light of significant litigation, large losses, or persistent customer dissatisfaction. The potential exposure may be increased by the number of accounts, the volume of assets under management, or the number of affected transactions. Management does not anticipate or take timely or appropriate actions in response to changes of a market or regulatory nature. Weaknesses may be observed in one or more critical operational, administrative, or investment activities. The institution's performance in self-policing risk is suspect. Management has either not initiated, or has a poor record of, corrective action to address problems.

Management information at various levels of the organization may exhibit significant weaknesses. Poor administration, conflicts of interest, and other legal or control breaches may be evident. Risk management processes, internal controls, or audit may be less than effective in reducing exposure.

Risk Matrix

Quality of Risk Management	Quantity of Risk		
	Low	**Moderate**	**High**
Weak	Moderate	High Moderate Quantity Precludes "Highest"	Highest
Satisfactory	Low Satisfactory Risk Management Precludes "Lowest"	Moderate	High Satisfactory Risk Management Precludes "Highest"
Strong	Lowest	Low Moderate Quantity Precludes "Lowest"	Moderate

Quantity of Risk

Note:

This matrix illustrates elements to consider in the risk decision process. The matrix represents how an aggregate risk assessment can be made based on the quantity of risk and the quality of risk management for each type of risk. When making the aggregate risk decision, however, examiners may consider other factors not depicted on this diagram.

Examiners can use a similar, one-dimensional risk matrix for composite risk decisions.

ROCA Rating System

ROCA, a management information and supervisory tool, rates the condition of an FBO's branch or agency and systematically identifies significant supervisory concerns at the branch or agency. ROCA stands for risk management, operational controls, compliance, and asset quality. For evaluation purposes, the rating system divides a branch's or agency's overall activities into three components: risk management, operational controls, and compliance. These components represent the major activities or processes of a branch or agency that may raise supervisory concern. The system also rates the quality of the branch's or agency's stock of assets as of the examination date.

ROCA replaces the rating system known as AIM (asset quality, internal controls, and management) because it better assesses the condition of a branch as part of an FBO. The new system is also better at pinpointing the key areas of supervisory concern in a branch or agency office.

Composite Rating

The overall or composite rating indicates whether, in the aggregate, the operations of the branch or agency may present supervisory concerns and the extent of any concerns. The composite rating should not be merely an arithmetic average of the component ratings; some components will often carry more weight than others. (For example, asset quality will carry more weight as the financial strength of the FBO weakens.) The examiner should assign and justify in the report a composite rating using the definitions provided below as a guide.

The composite rating is based on a scale from 1 (the least supervisory concern) through 5 (the most supervisory concern). The composite rating is defined as follows:

Composite Rating 1 • Branches and agencies in this group are strong in every respect. These branches and agencies require only normal supervisory attention.

Composite Rating 2 • Branches and agencies in this group are in satisfactory condition, but may have modest weaknesses that can be corrected by the branch's or agency's management in the normal course of business. Generally, they do not require additional or more than normal supervisory attention.

Composite Rating 3 • Branches and agencies in this group are in fair condition because of a combination of weaknesses in risk management, operational controls, and compliance, or asset quality problems that, in combination with the condition of the FBO or other factors, cause supervisory concern. In addition, the branch's or agency's management or head office management may not be taking the necessary corrective actions to address substantive weaknesses. This rating may also be assigned when risk management, operational controls, or compliance is individually viewed as unsatisfactory. Generally, these branches and agencies raise supervisory concern and require more than normal supervisory attention to address their weaknesses.

Composite Rating 4 • Branches and agencies in this group are in marginal condition because of serious weaknesses as reflected in the assessments of the individual components. Serious problems or unsafe and unsound banking practices or operations exist, which have not been satisfactorily addressed or resolved by the branch's or agency's management and/or head office management. Branches and agencies in this category require close supervisory attention and surveillance monitoring, as well as a definitive plan for corrective action by the branch's or agency's management and head office management.

Composite Rating 5 • Branches and agencies in this group are in unsatisfactory condition because of a high level of severe weaknesses or unsafe and unsound conditions and consequently require urgent restructuring of operations by the branch's or agency's management and head office management.

Disclosure

Following approval of the rating by appropriate senior supervisory officials at the examining agency, the composite and component numeric ratings should be disclosed in the "Examination Conclusions and Comments" section of the examination report. When the rating is disclosed, its meaning should be explained clearly using the appropriate composite and component rating definitions. The report should also make it clear that, as part of the overall findings of the examination, the rating is confidential.

Component Evaluations

Like the composite rating, the component ratings are evaluated on a scale from 1 to 5, 1 representing the lowest level of supervisory concern and 5 representing the highest. Each component is discussed below followed by a description of the individual performance ratings.

Risk Management

Every financial institution is exposed to risk. Risk management, or the process of identifying, measuring, and controlling risk, is an important responsibility of any financial institution. A branch or agency is typically removed from its head office by location and time zone; therefore, an effective risk management system is critical not only to manage the scope of its activities but to achieve comprehensive, ongoing oversight by local and head office management. Examiners should determine the extent to which risk management techniques enable local and head office management (1) to achieve and maintain oversight of the branch's or agency's activities and (2) to control risk exposures that result from the branch's or agency's activities.

The primary components of a sound risk management system are a comprehensive risk assessment approach; a detailed structure of limits and other guidelines that govern risk taking; and a strong management information system for monitoring and reporting risks.

In assessing risks, the branch or agency identifies each risk associated with its activities (both on and off the balance sheet) and groups them into risk categories. These categories broadly relate to credit, market, liquidity, operational, and legal risks.[1] All major risks should be measured explicitly and consistently by branch management, and they should be reevaluated on an ongoing basis as economic circumstances, market conditions, and the branch's or agency's activities change. The branch's or agency's expansion into new products or business lines should not outpace proper risk management or the head office's supervision. When risks cannot be explicitly measured, management should demonstrate knowledge of their potential impact and an ability to manage them.

---

[1] While operational risks are identified in the branch's or agency's overall risk assessment, the effectiveness of the branch's or agency's operational controls is evaluated separately.

Risk identification and measurement are followed by an evaluation of risks and returns to establish acceptable risk exposure levels. The branch's or agency's lending and trading policies establish these levels, subject to the approval of head office management. Policies should set standards for undertaking and evaluating risk exposure in individual branch or agency activities as well as procedures for tracking and reporting risk exposure to monitor compliance with established policy limits or guidelines.

Head office management has a role in developing and approving the branch's or agency's risk management system as part of its responsibility to provide a comprehensive system of oversight for the branch or agency. Generally, the branch's or agency's risk management system, including risk identification, measurement, limits or guidelines, and monitoring, should be modeled on that of the FBO. Doing so ensures a fully integrated, organization-wide risk management system.

In assigning the risk management rating, examiners should evaluate the branch's or agency's current situation, concentrating on developments since the previous examination. The rating should not concentrate on past problems, such as those relating to the current quality of the branch's or agency's stock of assets, if risk management techniques have improved significantly since those problems developed.[2]

A rating of 1 indicates that management has implemented a fully integrated risk management system. The system effectively identifies and controls all major types of risk at the branch or agency, including those from new products and the changing environment. This assessment, in most cases, will be supported by a superior level of financial performance and asset quality at the branch or agency. No supervisory concerns are evident.

A rating of 2 indicates that the risk management system is fully effective with respect to almost all major risk factors. It reflects a responsiveness and ability to cope successfully with existing and foreseeable exposures that may arise in carrying out the branch's or agency's business plan. While the branch or agency may have residual weaknesses from past exposures, its management or the head office's management is addressing these problems. Any such

---

[2]   Thus, for example, the change in the level of problem assets since the previous examination would normally be more important than the absolute level of problem assets. At the same time, a loan portfolio that has few borrowers experiencing debt service problems does not necessarily indicate a sound risk management system because underwriting standards may make the branch vulnerable to credit problems during a future economic downturn.

weaknesses will not have a material adverse effect on the branch or agency. Generally, risks are being controlled in a manner that does not require additional or greater-than-normal supervisory attention.

A rating of 3 signifies a risk management system that is lacking in some important respects. Its relative ineffectiveness in dealing with the branch's or agency's risk exposures is cause for greater-than-normal supervisory attention, and deterioration in financial performance indicators is probable. Current risk-related procedures are considered fair, existing problems are not being satisfactorily addressed, or risks are not being adequately identified and controlled. While these deficiencies may not have caused significant problems yet, there are clear indications that the branch or agency is vulnerable to risk-related deterioration.

A rating of 4 indicates a marginal risk management system that generally fails to identify and control significant risk exposures in many important respects. Generally, such circumstances reflect a lack of adequate guidance and supervision by head office management. As a result, deterioration in overall performance is imminent or is already evident in the branch's or agency's overall performance since the previous examination. Failure of management to correct risk management deficiencies that have created significant problems in the past warrants close supervisory attention.

A rating of 5 indicates that the branch or agency has critical performance problems that are due to the absence of an effective risk management system in almost every respect. Not only is there a large volume of problem risk exposures but the problems are also intensifying. Management has not demonstrated the ability to stabilize the branch's or agency's situation. If corrective actions are not taken immediately, the branch's or agency's ability to continue operating is in jeopardy.

Operational Controls

This component assesses the effectiveness of the branch's or agency's operational controls, including accounting and financial controls. Examiners expect branches and agencies to have an independent internal audit function, an adequate system of head office or external audits, or both. They should have a system of internal controls consistent with the size and complexity of their operations. Internal audit and control procedures should ensure that operations are conducted in accordance with internal guidelines and regulatory policies and that all reports and analyses provided to the head office and branch or agency senior management are comprehensive, timely, and accurate.

The OCC's supervision of a branch's or agency's operational controls has two basic goals. The first goal is to prevent branches and agencies participating in U.S. financial markets from undermining the high standards, efficiency, and confidence in the U.S. markets. The second goal is to ensure that head office management has adequate internal controls in place at the branch or agency (1) to ensure that the branch or agency is operating within corporate policies, and (2) to enable head office management, as well as the home country supervisor, to supervise the FBO on a consolidated basis in accordance with the supervisory principles of the Basle Committee on Banking Supervision.

A rating of 1 indicates that the branch or agency has a fully comprehensive system of operational controls that protects against losses from transactional and operational risks and ensures accurate financial reporting. In addition, branch or agency operations are fully consistent with sound market practices. The branch or agency also has a well-defined and independent audit function that is appropriate to the size and risk profile of the branch or agency. No supervisory concerns are evident.

A rating of 2 may indicate some minor weaknesses, such as modest control deficiencies caused by new business activities, that management is addressing. Some recommendations may be noted. Overall, the system of controls, including the audit function, is considered satisfactory and effective in maintaining a safe and sound branch or agency operation. Only routine supervisory attention is required.

A rating of 3 indicates that the branch's or agency's system of controls, including the quality of the audit function, is lacking in some important respects. Particular weakness is evidenced by continued control exceptions, substantial deficiencies in written policies and procedures, or the failure to adhere to written policies and procedures. As a result, greater-than-normal supervisory attention is required.

A rating of 4 signifies that the branch's or agency's system of operational controls has serious deficiencies that require substantial improvement. In such a case, the branch or agency may lack control functions, including those related to the audit function, that meet minimal expectations. Therefore, the branch's or agency's adherence to FBO and regulatory policies is questionable. Head office management has failed to give the branch or agency proper support to maintain operations in accordance with U.S. norms. Close supervisory attention is required.

A rating of 5 indicates that the branch's or agency's system of operational controls is so inadequate that its operations are in serious jeopardy. The branch or agency either lacks an audit function or has a wholly deficient one. The branch's or agency's management should improve operational controls immediately. Examiners should give the situation strong supervisory attention.

Compliance

Branches and agencies should demonstrate compliance with all applicable state and federal laws and regulations, including reporting and special supervisory requirements. To the extent possible, given the size and risk profile of the branch or agency, these responsibilities should be vested in a branch or agency official or compliance officer who is not a line manager and does not report to one. Branch or agency management should regularly ensure that all appropriate personnel are properly trained in meeting regulatory requirements. The audit function should be sufficient in scope to ensure that the branch or agency is meeting all applicable regulatory requirements.

A rating of 1 indicates an outstanding level of compliance with applicable laws, regulations, and reporting requirements. No supervisory concerns are evident.

A rating of 2 indicates that compliance is generally effective with respect to most factors. Compliance monitoring and related training programs are sufficient to prevent significant problems. Although minor reporting errors may be present, they are being adequately addressed by branch or agency management. Only normal supervisory attention is warranted.

A rating of 3 indicates that deficiencies in management and training systems have produced an atmosphere in which significant compliance problems could and do occur. Such deficiencies could include the lack of written compliance procedures, the absence of a system for identifying possible compliance issues, or a substantial number of minor or repeat violations or deficiencies. Greater-than-normal supervisory attention is warranted.

A rating of 4 indicates that the branch's or agency's and head office's management do not give compliance matters proper attention. Close supervisory attention is warranted. The branch or agency may not have an effective compliance program or an ongoing training program. It may fail to meet significant regulatory requirements, or its regulatory reports may contain significant, widespread inaccuracies.

A rating of 5 signals that the branch's or agency's attention to compliance matters is wholly lacking. Immediate supervisory attention is warranted.

Asset Quality

A national bank's asset quality is evaluated to determine whether it has sufficient capital to absorb prospective losses and, ultimately, whether it can maintain its viability as an ongoing enterprise. The evaluation of asset quality in a branch or agency does not have the same purpose because a branch or agency is not a separately capitalized entity. Instead, a branch's or agency's viability depends on the financial and managerial support of the FBO.

The ability of a branch or agency to honor its liabilities ultimately is based upon the FBO's condition and level of support from the FBO, a concept that is integral to the FBO Supervision Program. As indicated above, a branch or agency is not strictly limited by its own internal and external funding sources in meeting solvency and liquidity needs. Nonetheless, the evaluation of asset quality is important in assessing both the effectiveness of credit risk management and the ability of the branch's or agency's assets to pay liabilities and claims in a liquidation. (Generally, credit administration concerns should be addressed in rating the risk management component.)

In the OCC's FBO Supervision Program, an FBO whose financial condition is satisfactory is presumed to be able to support the branch or agency with sufficient capital and reserves on a consolidated basis. As a result, the assessment of asset quality in such circumstances would not be a predominant factor in the branch's or agency's overall assessment, if existing risk management techniques are satisfactory. If, however, the condition of the FBO is less than satisfactory and/or support from the FBO is questionable, the evaluation of asset quality should be carefully considered in determining whether supervisory actions are needed to improve the branch's or agency's ability to meet its obligations on a stand-alone basis. When a branch or agency is subject to asset maintenance, it is expected to address asset quality issues by removing classified assets from the list of eligible assets.

It may be appropriate for examiners to give the component for asset quality greater or lesser weight in a composite rating as the FBO's condition changes. For example, if the financial strength of the FBO weakens, the quality of assets booked in the United States becomes increasingly important as the source of protection for local creditors, and the "A" in ROCA should gain weight. Examiners may also choose to give the asset quality component more weight if the FBO's support for the branch or agency becomes questionable. But examiners should use their judgment in such circumstances. For example, a branch or agency that holds problem assets for other offices so that the FBO can better manage the workout process should not be penalized, so long as the FBO has the ability to support the level of problem assets. And when the FBO is strong and the need to look to local assets for protection of creditors seems remote, the quality of local assets is less important, and the "A" in ROCA should carry less weight.

A branch or agency accorded a rating of 1 has strong asset quality.

A branch or agency accorded a rating of 2 has satisfactory asset quality.

A branch or agency accorded a rating of 3 has fair asset quality.

A branch or agency accorded a rating of 4 has marginal asset quality.

A branch or agency accorded a rating of 5 has unsatisfactory asset quality.

Examiners supervising the U.S. operations of FBOs use the following terms:

Agreement Corporation — A corporation formed for the purpose of engaging in international banking, that has entered into an agreement with the Federal Reserve Board under which it will not exercise any power that is impermissible for an Edge Act Corporation. It may be licensed by the Federal Reserve Board or an individual state.

Asset Maintenance — The maintenance of a required percentage of eligible assets in a federal branch or agency. The asset maintenance required is calculated by dividing eligible assets by the federal branch's or agency's third-party liabilities. Third-party liabilities are obligations of the federal branch or agency to parties not connected with the FBO. Generally, these obligations do not include claims of the FBO's branches, subsidiaries, companies, or shareholders. Asset maintenance requirements are intended to preclude a federal branch or agency from being a net provider of funds to other parts of the FBO. The OCC may impose asset maintenance requirements on a federal branch or agency for prudential, supervisory, or enforcement reasons as circumstances warrant.

Commercial Lending Companies — State-licensed companies that make commercial loans and maintain credit balances. They do not accept deposits.

Edge Act Corporation — A corporation licensed by the Federal Reserve Board to engage in activities incidental to international business. "Edges" may accept deposits from foreign states, foreign persons, and certain other sources.

International Banking Facility — A set of asset and liability accounts segregated on the books and records of a depository institution, a U.S. branch or agency of a foreign bank, or an Edge corporation or Agreement corporation, that includes only international banking facility (IBF) time deposits and extensions of credit. IBFs allow U.S. depository institutions, U.S. offices of Edge and Agreement Corporations, and federal branches and agencies to conduct banking business with foreign residents in a regulatory environment broadly similar to that of an offshore branch (see below). In order to insulate U.S. economic activity from the transactions of IBFs, the Federal Reserve Board has imposed several restrictions on IBF activities. These restrictions:

- Prohibit lending to or accepting deposits from a U.S. resident other than the entity establishing the IBF or other IBFs.

- Prohibit the acceptance of transaction accounts.

- Prohibit the issuance of negotiable or bearer instruments.

- Require nonbank deposits to carry a minimum maturity or a required notice period of two business days. Bank deposits can be made with overnight maturities.

- Subject nonbank customer transactions to a minimum deposit or withdrawal amount of $100,000, except to close out an account or to withdraw accumulated interest.

- Require an IBF to notify its nonbank customers, in writing when first establishing an account relationship, that (1) the deposits received by the IBF may be used only to support its operations outside the United States, and (2) extensions of credit by the IBF may be used only to finance the customers' operations outside the United States. When customers are foreign affiliates of U.S. residents, the IBF is required to obtain the customers' acknowledgment that they have received such notice.

Limited Federal Branch — An FBO's office, licensed by the OCC, that can exercise in full all but one of a federal branch's powers. A limited branch can accept only such deposits as would be permissible for an Edge Act Corporation (it cannot accept deposits from U.S. citizens or corporations).

Offshore Branch — A non-U.S. branch established in an offshore center. It may also be referred to as a "shell branch" because it often does not have a physical presence and is only nominally domiciled in the offshore center. FBOs are able to use offshore centers to conduct a banking business free of any U.S. reserve requirements or FDIC premiums.

Representative Offices — A foreign bank's offices other than its branches, agencies, or subsidiaries (12 CFR 211.21). These offices, which can be located in any state, are licensed and supervised by the states and the Federal Reserve Board. They may engage in marketing, loan production, and research.

Third-party Liabilities — Any liabilities of the branch or agency with persons or entities that are not related parties or affiliates of the FBO or other offices of the parent bank.

Law

12 USC 3101 et seq., International Banking Act

Regulation

12 CFR 28, International Banking Activities

Issuances

Policies and Procedures Manual (PPM) 5500-1, "Communications with Foreign Bank Supervisors"